# BEER HIKING PENNSYLVANIA AND NEW JERSEY

The Tastiest Way to Discover the Beaches, Mountains, and Cities of the Northern Mid-Atlantic

**Beer Hiking Pennsylvania and New Jersey**
The Tastiest Way to Discover the Beaches, Mountains, and Cities of the Northern Mid-Atlantic

By: Hannah Powell

ISBN: 978-3-03964-062-1
Published by Helvetiq, Lausanne/Basel, Switzerland
Graphic Design and illustration: Daniel Malak, Jędrzej Malak (maps)
Printed in China
First Edition March 2025


info@helvetiq.ch

www.helvetiq.com/us
www.facebook.com/helvetiq_usa
instagram: @helvetiq_usa

HEL·VETIQ helvetiq.com

MIX
Paper from responsible sources
FSC® C167893
www.fsc.org

# BEER HIKING PENNSYLVANIA AND NEW JERSEY

The Tastiest Way to Discover the Beaches, Mountains, and Cities of the Northern Mid-Atlantic

# TABLE OF CONTENTS

# 1

# INTRODUCTION

# ABOUT THE AUTHOR

Hannah Powell is a beer enthusiast, hiker, and trail running junkie. After years of grabbing a craft beer after hiking, in 2021 she started her blog Hikes & Hops to share her many hikes and brewery recommendations with others. Born and raised in Pittsburgh, Pennsylvania, one could say she's been researching this book her whole life (though she officially began in 2023) and is excited to share all the wonderful trails and craft breweries in her home state and beyond.

An outdoors lover since childhood, Hannah caught the hiking bug while living in Scotland for graduate school. Although she unwisely undertook her first major trek up Beinn Dubh in the Scottish Highlands in a pair of wellies, hiking quickly became a new favorite hobby. Now equipped with the right footwear, she's spent most weekends over the last few years on the trails—though sometimes her hikes take longer than expected because she's too busy looking at mushrooms and learning tree facts! From national parks to local county trails, she loves to explore well-known treasures and hidden gems alike. In addition to hiking, she's recently joined a wonderful trail running community and has tackled the 37-mile Rachel Carson Trail Challenge.

Hannah was introduced to the world of craft beer when her dad, a homebrewer, took her to a local Pittsburgh brewery for her first legal beer. Much to her wallet's chagrin, after that first pint, she immediately developed a taste for craft beer. Even more than a love for the beer itself, she found herself drawn to the community surrounding craft brewing and how these small businesses often become beloved institutions in their local neighborhoods. Although she doesn't limit herself to any particular beer styles, Hannah will never turn down an oatmeal stout and is fond of "front porch" wheat ales.

Hannah and her partner Justin live in Pittsburgh where they spend most weekends in the woods and taking on far too many DIY projects.

You can find her on Instagram @hikesandhopsblog and at hikesandhops.org.

# ABOUT BEER HIKING IN PENNSYLVANIA AND NEW JERSEY

The sprawling forests of Pennsylvania and New Jersey make hiking one of the most popular outdoor activities in the region. These two Mid-Atlantic states offer a wide range of landscapes including rocky mountain overlooks, old-growth forests, pine barrens, glacial boulder fields, river gorges, and sandy beaches. They're united by the Appalachian Mountains, which span from Pennsylvania's southern border up through New Jersey's northern edge. For those hikers who enjoy kicking back with a post-hike brew, you'll find a wealth of options in the region's thriving craft beer industry; the combined states boast over 600 craft breweries, so you're sure to find a pint for every palate.

New Jersey is the most densely populated state in the nation, with nearly 90% of New Jersey's population living within 50 miles of the metro centers of NYC and Philadelphia. However, the aptly named "Garden State" is also home to nearly 2 million acres of forested lands including popular state and national parks. The Appalachian Mountain highlands and miles of Atlantic shoreline prove it's far more than just a suburb of New York City. In the north, the Delaware Water Gap and Appalachian Mountains form a rocky region chock full of waterfalls, markedly different from the southern sprawling pine barrens and sandy beaches. Although relatively new to the craft beer craze, breweries are flourishing in New Jersey with most focusing on small-batch barrels and locally-sourced ingredients.

Founded by the colonial Quaker, William Penn, Pennsylvania fittingly means "Penn's Woods" as the state has millions of acres of protected forest for public use. The robust state park and forest system is free for all users, regardless of residency. Pennsylvania is bordered by six states with a small shoreline along Lake Erie in its northwestern corner. The urban centers of Pittsburgh and Philadelphia bookend the state with the Laurel Highlands, Allegheny National Forest, and Pocono Mountains being just a few of the natural regions stretching in between. The mighty Delaware River forms the entirety of the border between Pennsylvania and New Jersey before spilling into the Delaware Bay. Boasting the second highest number of breweries of any state in the country, Pennsylvania has boundless opportunities for beer buffs to find a locally made brew.

Within the pages of this book, you'll find a route for every hiker, from strenuous mountain climbs to relaxing lakeside rambles. Whether it's birdwatching in Cape May or rock scrambling on the Appalachian Trail, you'll be blown away by the natural beauty of Pennsylvania and New Jersey. Across both states, you're sure to find a local craft taproom serving creative and distinctly regional takes on the age-old brewing tradition. From beer gardens to tap houses, there's nothing more satisfying than a fresh, locally crafted brew to toast your fruitful sojourn in nature.

# CHOOSE THE BEER OR THE HIKE

HIKE LOCATION

REGION

MAP

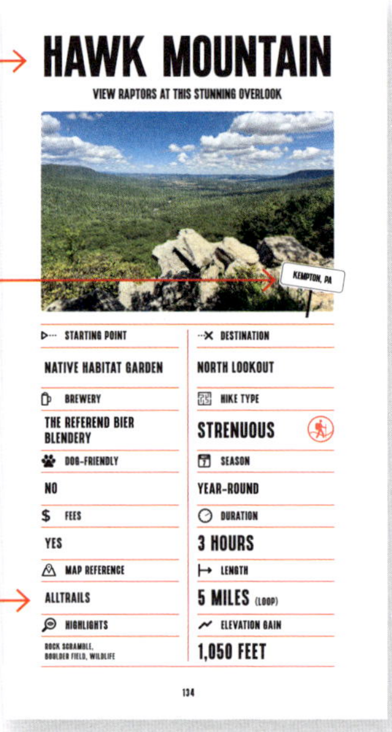


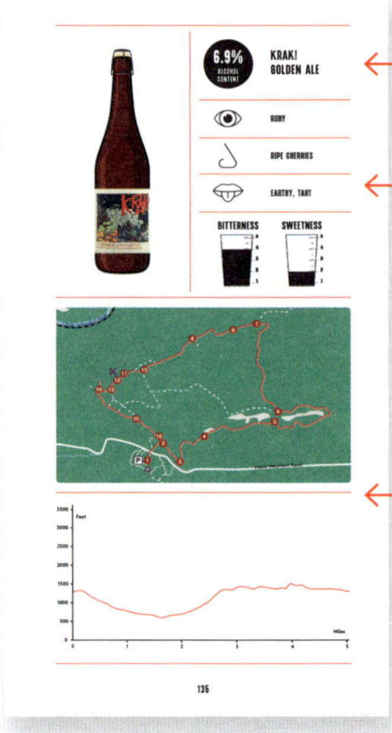


NAME OF THE BEER

INFORMATION ABOUT THE BEER

INFORMATION ABOUT THE HIKE

# ON THE HIKES AND HIKE RATINGS

All of these hikes are carefully selected to showcase the best of the natural region of Pennsylvania and New Jersey. The hikes fall into three categories of difficulty: Easy, Moderate, and Strenuous. The majority of the hikes are rated Moderate.

## EASY

The terrain is mostly flat and frequently on wide, paved, or gravel paths. Generally these hikes have less than 200 feet of elevation and clock in under three miles. They are great for beginners and families but can be enjoyed by all hikers.

## MODERATE

The terrain is typically single-track natural trails that often have rocky or uneven footing. They usually gain between 200 to 900 feet of elevation and range between three to five miles. There may be some minor technical spots like steep inclines or light rock clambering.

## STRENUOUS

These are longer hikes with significant elevation gain. There may be some challenging sections with rock scrambles or creek crossings. Some strenuous hikes are rated thus simply for mileage, while others are shorter but feature difficult inclines. These hikes should only be undertaken by experienced hikers.

The hikes are broken down by type of hike; either a round trip, which follows the same path out and back, or a loop, which makes some form of loop without backtracking. All of the hikes begin and end at the same location, and all have available parking for at least several cars. Also, each hike notes whether it's dog-friendly. For all of the included hike information, always double-check regulations before heading out to ensure nothing has changed.

All of the hikes include an approximate length of time to complete. Remember that this is just an estimation; you may take shorter or longer to complete the route depending on hiking speed, weather condition, experience level, and time for snack breaks and photo ops.

Many of the hikes take place in state parks, which are free in Pennsylvania. One Pennsylvania hike takes place at a nonprofit where there is a small entrance fee. There is a nominal fee to use New Jersey State Parks which varies at each location and has a reduced rate for New Jersey residents. Consider purchasing an annual State Park Pass, which provides unlimited access to all New Jersey State Parks. Other hikes take place in New Jersey county parks which are free.

# ON THE BREWERIES AND BEER RATINGS

Pennsylvania and New Jersey offer a unique perspective on the nation's brewing tradition. Pennsylvania has a huge number of breweries, second only to California. New Jersey has been a late-comer to the brewing renaissance, with strict state regulations constraining the budding craft brewery scene. Now however, with recent loosening of restrictions, craft breweries are blossoming in the Garden State.

The breweries highlighted in this book are all selected for a variety of factors, including proximity to the trailhead, taproom hours, personal experience, and recommendations from fellow beer hikers. There are only so many breweries that can be included in a book like this, so there are regrettably a few wonderful establishments that didn't make the cut. This book aims to showcase the wide range of regional breweries from industry veterans to hidden gems. Wherever possible, I prioritized breweries owned and operated by women and minorities, because craft beer, like the great outdoors, is for everybody. Some breweries offer food, while others have food trucks or allow you to bring snacks. Many featured breweries are small operations, so it's always a good idea to double-check operating hours before heading out. Several breweries are dog-friendly, while others prefer you leave your pooch at home.

The taproom locations are as diverse as the region itself. You'll find breweries on farms, in industrial parks, on main streets, and even at airfields. You'll meet brewers producing traditional styles, while others experiment with unique flavors. Most of the breweries are accessed by car, so always be responsible while beer hiking and never put yourself and others at risk by driving while impaired.

The featured beer is often the flagship beer or the most popular offering. Sometimes, it's a unique style or flavor that's only available in that particular area. In many cases, the featured beer is named after a trail or landscape enjoyed on your hike. Most of the featured beers are available year-round, while some are seasonal offerings. A handful of the breweries have rotating taplists where there is always something new on the menu, in which case, the featured beer was simply a favorite brew offered at the time of visiting. The featured beers represent a wide variety of flavors rather than focusing on a single style. IPAs feature heavily due to their persistent popularity, but you'll also find sours, stouts, lagers, and more. All of the beer ratings are subjective and based on my own interpretation. Your experience may be different!

# PREPARING FOR YOUR HIKE

## THE TEN ESSENTIALS (AND THEN SOME)

No matter the type of hike, it's always important to be prepared when hitting the trails.

- **Navigation.** The maps in this book are meant for reference only. Although there are many watches and phone apps to help navigate, batteries die and technology can malfunction. It's always a good idea to have a paper map, a compass, and the knowledge of how to use them.
- **Sun protection.** Even in the woods, you are susceptible to punishing sun rays. Always have sunglasses, a hat, and sunscreen. Remember, you can get sunburned even in the winter!
- **Insulation.** Temperatures at overlooks and mountain peaks can be wildly different from those at the trailhead. Always have an extra layer in case of cold or unexpected precipitation. An extra pair of dry socks can prevent major discomfort after stream crossings.
- **Illumination.** Whether catching an early sunrise or when sunset comes sooner than expected, you should always carry a flashlight or headlamp with you. And don't forget the batteries!
- **First Aid Supplies.** Hiking comes with some risks, and it's best to be prepared for injuries. Carry a small first aid kit and know how to handle minor injuries. Always check your supplies and make sure to replace expired items.
- **Firestarter.** Fire can be a heat source, used for cooking, and even as an emergency signal. Carry waterproof matches in a sealed container and make sure you know how to start a fire. Always be familiar with the fire regulations in your area.
- **Tools.** A handy multi-tool can go a long way on the trail. Also, a whistle can draw attention in case of an emergency.
- **Nutrition.** No one wants their energy levels to crash mid-hike. Always pack extra trail-friendly snacks or even a full lunch for a long day of hiking. Make sure to have more than you think you need.
- **Hydration.** Carrying water is a must while hiking, especially in the summer humidity. Always carry more than you think you'll need and have extra water in the car for your return. Proper hydration is essential for preventing heat stroke and other heat-related illnesses.
- **Shelter.** During an unexpected overnight, some form of shelter, even just a small tarp or space blanket, could be life-saving.
- **Insect protection.** Incessant bugs can quickly change a fun hike into a miserable slog. Bug spray can protect from ticks. Carry a mosquito net to protect your face from biting insects.

## HIKING SEASON

Hiking can be enjoyed year-round as long as you are adequately prepared. Each season brings its rewards and challenges. Spring brings wildflowers as well as heavy rains that can leave muddy, washed out trails. Summer's longer days offer more daylight for hitting the trails, but you'll have to contend with high temperatures and humidity. Fall is an ideal time for hiking with cooler days, but as prime hiking season, you'll likely be sharing the trail with other fall foliage enjoyers. Winter hiking offers fewer crowds on popular trails, but proper preparation is necessary for tackling snowy trails and freezing temperatures. It's always a good idea to check trail conditions before heading out and never venture out when conditions are hazardous.

## HUNTING SEASONS

Hunting season in New Jersey and Pennsylvania vary greatly depending on season, animal, and weapon. Hunting seasons can extend from September to February, although it's generally not permitted on Sundays. It's always recommended to wear bright orange while hiking during fall and winter. You should also consult local hunting regulations for specific details before heading out.

New Jersey Fish and Wildlife, dep.nj.gov/njfw
Pennsylvania Game Commission, pgc.pa.gov

## WEATHER

The weather fluctuates greatly across Pennsylvania and New Jersey. Generally, expect to encounter hot and humid summers and cold, snowy winters. Areas of high elevation like the Appalachian Mountains experience cooler temperatures and more snowfall than others. Heavy thunderstorms are frequent in the late summer throughout the region, but mild spring and fall temperatures make for ideal hiking conditions. Weather conditions can change rapidly, so always be prepared. For accurate weather forecasts, visit the National Weather Service at weather.gov.

# ADDITIONAL RESOURCES

## PENNSYLVANIA

### Hiking
AllTrails, alltrails.com
PA State Parks, dcnr.pa.gov/StateParks
Keystone Trails Association, kta-hike.org

### Breweries
Brewers of PA, brewersofpa.org
Breweries in PA, breweriesinpa.com

### Visitor Amenities
Visit PA, visitpa.com

## NEW JERSEY

### Hiking
AllTrails, alltrails.com
NJ Hiking, njhiking.com
NJ State Parks, nj.gov/dep/parksandforests

### Breweries
New Jersey Craft Beer, newjerseycraftbeer.com
New Jersey Brewer's Guild, brewersguildnj.com

### Visitor Amenities
Visit NJ, visitnj.org

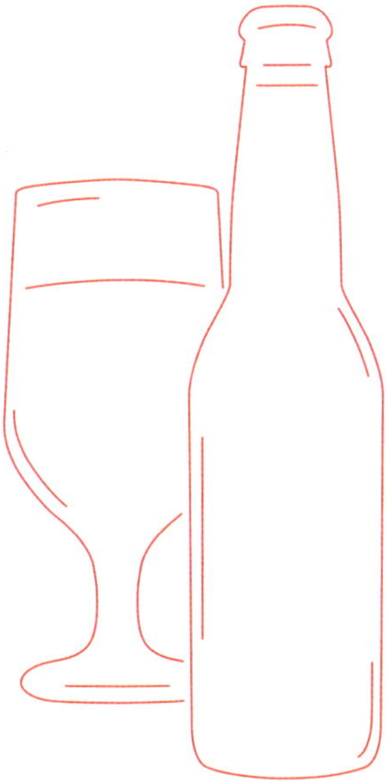

# TRAIL ETIQUETTE

Enjoying the great outdoors is quite literally, as easy as a walk in the park, so it's no wonder that hiking is seeing a spike in popularity. The only things you truly need to enjoy a day walking in nature are the Ten Essentials and a good attitude. For that reason, while enjoying a hike, it's not uncommon to see the full range of hikers pass you by on the trail, from young to old, fast to slow, newbie to veteran. While some of the hikes in this book are hidden gems, quite a few traverse more popular trails. No matter the trail, it's important that we're all respectful hikers and proactive land stewards. Following the rules of trail etiquette will ensure that you, those around you, and future generations can have a pleasant time in the great outdoors.

- **Stay on the trail.** Avoid stepping off the trail unless yielding. This prevents erosion and damage to plant life. Always walk through mud, not around it.
- **Pack out trash.** Carry a plastic bag for packing out your garbage (and other trash found on trail). Never leave trash on the trail, even compostable trash like fruit peels which can attract pests and stink up the trail.
- **Limit group size.** Many parks limit group size to twelve. Larger groups can negatively impact the environment and the enjoyment of other hikers. If hiking with a large group, consider splitting into smaller groups and plan to meet up afterward.
- **Leave nature as you found it.** Do not disturb nature. As you've heard: "Take only photos, leave only footprints." Don't take souvenirs. Don't move rocks in waterways.
- **Practice good bathroom hygiene.** When nature calls, go at least 200 feet away from the trail and any water source. Bury waste in a cathole and pack out any toilet paper.
- **Be considerate of other hikers.** Everyone wants to enjoy their time in nature. Be considerate by greeting other hikers and keeping a friendly atmosphere on the trail. Allow the sounds of nature to prevail by keeping voices low and avoid music or phone calls. Always make yourself known to others hikers to avoiding surprises.
- **Yield to uphill hikers.** Hikers going uphill have the right of way. Hikers should always yield to horses. Mountain bikers technically

should yield to hikers, but often it's difficult for them to stop going downhill, so it's helpful to yield to bikers by stepping to the side where possible.

- **Park responsibly at the trailhead.** Park only in designated spots. If the trailhead is full, come back another time. Plan to do popular hikes at off-peak times and seasons. Always lock your vehicle and never leave valuables in the car.
- **Hike responsibly with pets.** When hiking on pet-friendly trails, always keep dogs on a short leash and under control at all times. Always bag and pack out animal waste.
- **Be aware of wildlife.** When hiking in nature, you may find yourself encountering the rich wildlife of the region. Generally, the animals will not bother you as long as you give them space. Be aware that the forests of Pennsylvania and New Jersey are home to some species that may be dangerous to hikers including black bears, coyotes, rattlesnakes, and elk. Usually, these animals are more afraid of you, but it's a good rule of thumb to make some noise while hiking and always be aware of your surroundings. Never feed or approach any wildlife.

# 2

# MAP & INDEX

# MAP

**WESTERN PENNSYLVANIA**

1. Frick Park
2. Raccoon Creek Wildflower Reserve
3. Slippery Rock Gorge
4. Glacier Ridge Trail
5. Ferncliff Peninsula
6. Adam Falls and Flat Rock
7. Presque Isle State Park
8. Forest Cathedral

**CENTRAL PENNSYLVANIA**

9. Kinzua Bridge
10. Mount Nittany
11. Hawk Rock
12. Wildwood Park
13. Pine Creek Gorge
14. Smith Knob

EASTERN PENNSYLVANIA
15. Salt Springs
16. Ricketts Glen
17. Shades of Death
18. Hawk Mountain
19. Kelly's Run
20. High Rocks Vista
21. Ridley Creek
22. Valley Forge
23. Wissahickon Valley Park
NORTHERN NEW JERSEY
24. High Point State Park
25. Stairway to Heaven
26. Buttermilk Falls
27. Mount Tammany
28. Schooley's Mountain Preserve
29. South Mountain Reservation
30. Devil's Half Acre
SOUTHERN NEW JERSEY
31. Cheesequake State Park
32. Hartshorne Woods Park
33. Batsto Lake
34. Maurice River Bluffs
35. Cape May Point
VT
MA
CT
NJ
DE
NEW YORK
PHILADELPHIA
Atlantic Ocean

# HIKES

| HIKE | CITY, STATE | LENGTH | PAGE |
|---|---|---|---|
| Adam Falls and Flat Rock | Rector, PA | 2.2 miles | 58 |
| Batsto Lake | Hammonton, NJ | 4.2 miles | 228 |
| Buttermilk Falls and Crater Lake Loop | Walpack Township, NJ | 6.1 miles | 184 |
| Cape May Point | Cape May, NJ | 2.2 miles | 240 |
| Cheesequake State Park | Matawan, NJ | 4.0 miles | 216 |
| Devil's Half-Acre | Hillsborough Township, NJ | 5.6 miles | 208 |
| Ferncliff Peninsula | Ohiopyle, PA | 1.8 miles | 52 |
| Forest Cathedral | Cooksburg, PA | 1.6 miles | 70 |
| Frick Park | Pittsburgh, PA | 5.2 miles | 28 |
| Glacier Ridge Trail | Portersville, PA | 7.3 miles | 46 |
| Hartshorne Woods Park | Highlands, NJ | 3.3 miles | 222 |
| Hawk Mountain | Kempton, PA | 5 miles | 134 |
| Hawk Rock | Duncannon, PA | 1.6 miles | 90 |
| High Point State Park | Montague, NJ | 3.7 miles | 172 |
| High Rocks Vista | Pipersville, PA | 3.5 miles | 146 |
| Kellys Run | Holtwood, PA | 3.7 miles | 140 |
| Kinzua Bridge | Kane, PA | 1.5 miles | 78 |
| Maurice River Bluffs | Millville, NJ | 5.0 miles | 234 |
| Mount Nittany | State College, PA | 4.7 miles | 84 |
| Mount Tammany | Columbia, NJ | 3.7 miles | 190 |
| Pine Creek Gorge | Wellsboro, PA | 3 miles | 102 |
| Presque Isle State Park | Erie, PA | 3.1 miles | 64 |
| Raccoon Creek Wildflower Reserve | Clinton, PA | 2.4 miles | 34 |
| Ricketts Glen State Park | Shickshinny, PA | 4.1 miles | 122 |
| Ridley Creek State Park | Media, PA | 4.6 miles | 152 |
| Salt Springs Waterfalls | Montrose, PA | 2 miles | 116 |
| Schooley's Mountain Park | Long Valley, NJ | 2.4 miles | 196 |
| Shades of Death | Carbon County, PA | 2.6 miles | 128 |
| Slippery Rock Gorge | Portersville, PA | 14.2 miles | 40 |
| Smith Knob | Williamsport, PA | 4.5 miles | 108 |
| South Mountain Reservation | West Orange, NJ | 5.1 miles | 202 |
| Stairway to Heaven | Vernon, NJ | 6.8 miles | 178 |
| Valley Forge | Valley Forge, PA | 4 miles | 158 |
| Wildwood Park | Harrisburg, PA | 3.2 miles | 96 |
| Wissahickon Valley Park | Philadelphia, PA | 5.1 miles | 164 |

# BREWERIES & BEERS

# 3

# THE BEER HIKES

# WESTERN PENNSYLVANIA

# FRICK PARK

## PITTSBURGH'S URBAN WOODLAND

| STARTING POINT | DESTINATION |
|---|---|
| ENVIRONMENTAL CENTER | NINE-MILE RUN BOARDWALK |
| BREWERY | HIKE TYPE |
| EAST END BREWING CO. | MODERATE |
| DOG-FRIENDLY | SEASON |
| YES (LEASH REQUIRED) | YEAR-ROUND |
| FEES | DURATION |
| NONE | 2 HOURS |
| MAP REFERENCE | LENGTH |
| ALLTRAILS | 5.2 MILES (LOOP) |
| HIGHLIGHTS | ELEVATION GAIN |
| CREEK, LAWN BOWLING, NATURE CENTER | 550 FEET |

**4.7%**
**ALCOHOL CONTENT**

## PEDAL PALE ALE

**CLEAR GOLD**

**HOPPY, BREADY**

**GRAPEFRUIT, FLORAL**

**BITTERNESS**

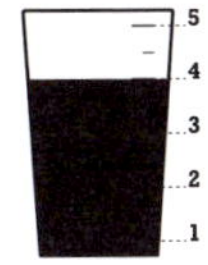


**SWEETNESS**

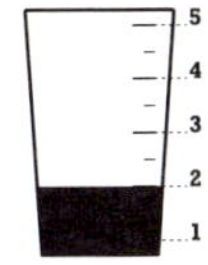

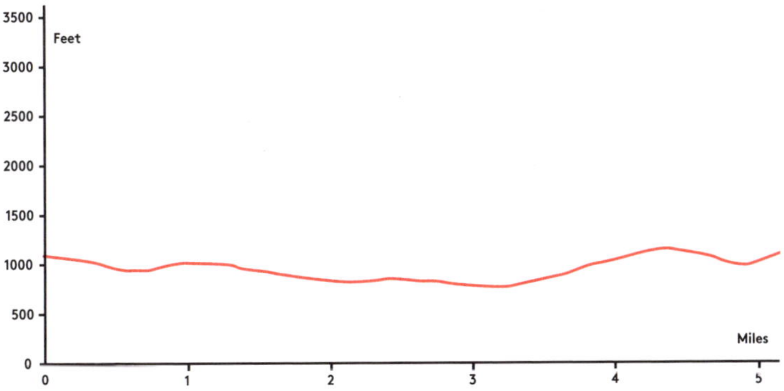

# HIKE DESCRIPTION

**Take this perimeter loop to explore history and sustainability in Pittsburgh's urban woodland. After, head a few miles down the road to East End Brewing, a pioneer in Pittsburgh's craft brewing scene.**

You'll start your journey at the historic gatehouse and the Environmental Center, from which you'll hike down a wooded trail, across a ravine, and past cottages built into hillsides. After around 1 mile, you'll emerge onto a greenway with public lawn bowling fields.

Past the lawn bowling fields, you'll see the Frick Museum and Historical Center to the right. This museum sits on the grounds of the Frick family mansion in Pittsburgh. Henry Clay Frick, wealthy businessman and co-founder of the US Steel Corporation, bequeathed a parcel of land near his home to use as a public park. This land became Frick Park, which opened to the public in 1927. Over the years, it has grown to over 600 acres, making it Pittsburgh's largest park.

Leaving the historical center behind, you'll pass the century-old gatehouse designed by renowned architect John Russell Smith. From here, you'll take a peaceful stroll among towering sycamores, black walnut trees, wildflowers, and songbirds along the aptly named Tranquil Trail. While walking through this green wonderland, it's easy to see why Frick is known as Pittsburgh's urban woodland. Eventually, you'll take wooden steps on the left to access a single-track route rambling over roots and rocks along a wooded hillside.

After leaving the gently rolling trail, you'll start on the Nine-Mile Run boardwalk. This waterway runs along a former slag dump. In Pittsburgh's industrial heyday, a waste product of the steel-making industry called slag was dumped along the creek bed. Over the decades, harmful chemicals leaked from the industrial waste and left Nine-Mile Run inhabitable to wildlife. The park underwent a huge restoration effort in the early 2000s to clean up the water. Today, the area is revitalized and beavers once again call the river home.

At the end of the boardwalk, you'll follow the Iron Gate Trail up challenging switchbacks in the densest part of the woods. You'll emerge from the woods onto the paved Riverview Trail. To the left is a playground with a large, blue slide built into the hillside. Made famous by rapper and Pittsburgh native Mac Miller, Blue Slide Park is popular with kids and adults alike. In a few hundred feet, you'll head back into the woods on the Bench Trail, another lightly-traveled, wooded trail.

Your hike ends by ascending a shallow ravine and set of steps beside the Environmental Center back to the park entrance. Take a moment to appreciate the Center's beauty, which opened in 2015 as a LEED-certified building. It's free to visit and offers educational programs and exhibits about nature and sustainability.

## TURN-BY-TURN DIRECTIONS

1. From the main entrance, pass the native plant garden and bathrooms on the left, then head into the woods on the unmarked wide gravel path to the left.
2. At 0.4 miles, turn left to follow the trail down to the road. Use the crosswalk to cross the street and then turn right and cross the bridge.
3. At 0.6 miles, turn left onto the gravel path between stone columns. In 200 feet, the gravel path joins a narrow road. Continue straight on the road.
4. At 0.8 miles, turn left onto the signposted Rosemary Trail to go back into the woods.
5. At 0.9 miles, the Rosemary Trail ends on a wide gravel path. Turn left and follow the path.
6. At 1.0 miles, turn left to stay on the Rosemary Trail. Do not head into the neighborhood. The lawn bowling fields will be on the right.
7. At 1.3 miles, pass the Reynolds Street Gatehouse and stay left to get on the marked Tranquil Trail. In 200 feet, turn left to follow the trail into the dense woods.

8. At 2.3 miles, at the trail intersection, turn left to leave the Tranquil Trail. Continue for 200 feet, then take the wooden steps up. At the top of the steps, turn right onto the Braddock Trail.
9. At 2.4 miles, after crossing the park street, take the lower trail to get on the Dinky Bridge Trail.
10. At 2.8 miles, turn right to continue down the marked Dinky Bridge Trail.
11. At 2.9 miles, at the T-intersection, turn right to get on the wide flat path. In 100 feet, turn left onto the marked Nine-Mile Run Boardwalk.
12. At 3.3 miles, the boardwalk ends. Turn right onto a gravel trail, ignoring a parking lot straight ahead.
13. At 3.4 miles, at the four-way intersection, stay straight to take the Iron Gate Trail, leaving the wide trail and heading into denser woods.
14. At 4.2 miles, turn right at the four-way intersection.
15. At 4.3 miles, emerge onto the paved Riverview Trail. Turn right and continue for 250 feet before turning left into the woods on the Bench Trail.
16. At 4.8 miles, the Bench Trail ends at the large trail intersection. Turn left to cross the bridge, then left again to start on the Falls Ravine Trail.
17. At 5.1 miles, take the stairs on the left to ascend beside the Environmental Center. At the top of the steps, the main park entrance is to the left.

## FIND THE TRAILHEAD

From downtown Pittsburgh, take Bigelow Boulevard east. In 2.4 miles, make a slight left at the traffic light onto North Craig Street. In 0.2 miles, turn left at the traffic light onto Baum Boulevard. In 0.4 miles, turn right at the light onto Morewood Avenue. After 0.5 miles, at the light, turn left onto Fifth Avenue. In 0.3 miles, turn right onto Wilkins Avenue and then proceed for 1.1 miles. At the light, turn right onto Beechwood Boulevard. The park entrance will be on the left in 0.9 miles. There is parking to the left of the large stone gates. Return to the gates to begin the hike.

# EAST END BREWING CO.

East End Brewing Co. has been a staple of the Pittsburgh beer scene for over two decades. In 2004, owner Scott Smith took a leap of faith and left his full-time corporate job to take his homebrewing hobby to the next level. Beginning as a production brewery, Scott and longtime head brewer Brendan Benson now operate two permanent taprooms and a seasonal pop-up.

True to the name, Scott and Brendon have been operating in the East End of Pittsburgh since the very beginning. Besides the fantastic line-up of house-made brews, visitors can snag a bite from "East End Chewing," the in-house pizza parlor.

In 2019, Scott and Brendon launched the popular "You Are Here" series. The series celebrates Pittsburgh by devoting a specially brewed beer to each of its 90 distinct neighborhoods. Released with a launch in the featured neighborhood, the beers give the brewery and beer lovers a chance to explore new areas of town, each with its quirky identity.

The popular Pedal Pale Ale is a light, easy-drinking ale that coasts into the taproom just in time for warmer weather. Pedal Ale season kicks off with the annual Keg Ride for charity. Hundreds of beer-loving cyclists follow kegs of the ale to a secret location in Pittsburgh where Scott taps the kegs and all enjoy the fresh brew.

## LAND MANAGER

**Pittsburgh Citiparks**
414 Grant Street
Pittsburgh, PA 15219
(412) 255-2539
pittsburghpa.gov/citiparks/beta/index.html
Map: storymaps.arcgis.com/stories/5ccb1bdc9b-1c424aa506dd276379fb0e?cover=true

## BREWERY/RESTAURANT

**East End Brewing Co.**
147 Julius Street
Pittsburgh, PA 15206
(412) 537-2337
eastendbrewing.com

Distance from trailhead: 2.2 miles

# RACCOON CREEK WILDFLOWER RESERVE

## STROLL AMONG 700 SPECIES OF NATIVE WILDFLOWERS

| STARTING POINT | DESTINATION |
|---|---|
| WILDFLOWER RESERVE INTERPRETIVE CENTER | RACCOON CREEK |
| **BREWERY** | **HIKE TYPE** |
| FERMATA BREWING COMPANY | EASY |
| **DOG-FRIENDLY** | **SEASON** |
| NO | YEAR-ROUND |
| **FEES** | **DURATION** |
| NONE | 1 HOUR |
| **MAP REFERENCE** | **LENGTH** |
| POSTED AT TRAILHEAD | 2.4 MILES (LOOP) |
| **HIGHLIGHTS** | **ELEVATION GAIN** |
| WILDFLOWERS, HISTORIC CABIN | 164 FEET |

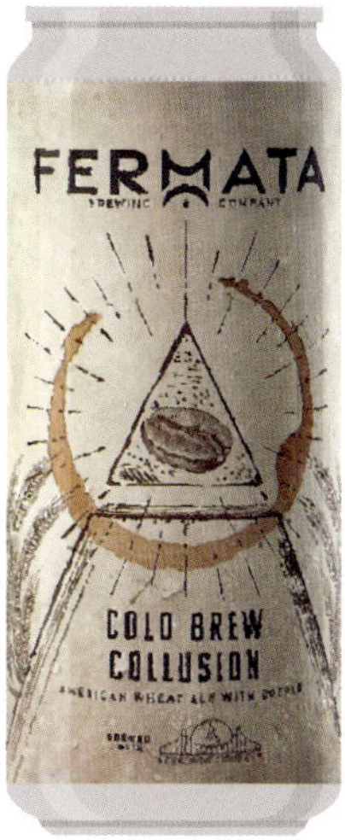


5.3% ALCOHOL CONTENT

# COLD BREW COLLUSION COFFEE WHEAT

CLEAR GOLD

FRESHLY BREWED COFFEE

BREADY WITH A HINT OF COFFEE

BITTERNESS

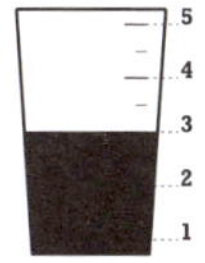


SWEETNESS

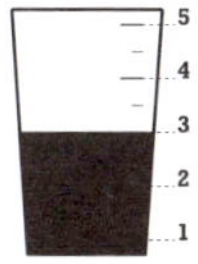


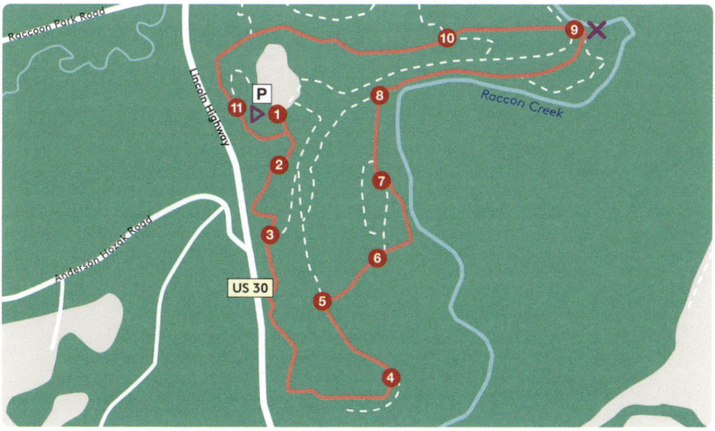


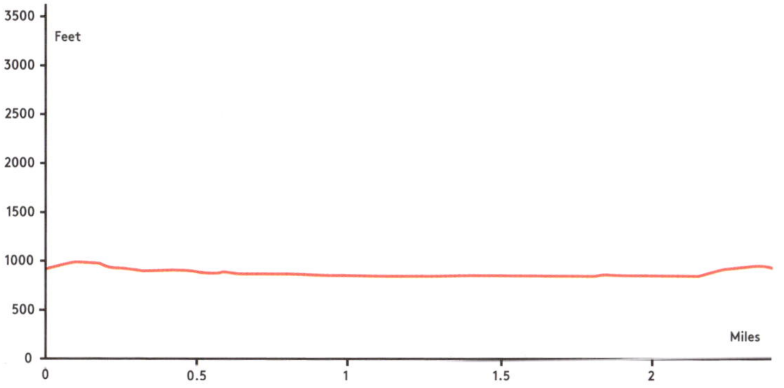

# HIKE DESCRIPTION

**Explore an abundance of native wildflowers along tranquil trails at this creekside reserve. Afterward, get your groove on at the musically-inclined Fermata Brewing on the main street of Ambridge.**

The Wildflower Reserve, nestled into the eastern side of the 7,500-acre Raccoon Creek State Park, is a haven for native plants. It contains one of the most biodiverse fields of wildflowers in the entire state. While visitors can enjoy the reserve all year, these trails are best in late spring and early fall when the wildflowers are in full bloom. The hike isn't very long or challenging, but you may want to dedicate a full half-day to immerse yourself in this tranquil landscape.

To begin, head to the trail kiosk at the end of the parking lot to study some pictures and descriptions of some of the many wildflowers that you could see on this hike. Then, you'll set out on the Old Jennings Trail. All of the trails at the Wildflower Reserve are color-coded, and blazes appear on trees and signposts at trail intersections to guide your way. Many of the trail names in the reserve draw from pioneering biologists in Pittsburgh who specialized in wildflowers.

After heading up the hill on the Jennings Trail, you'll reach a clearing with a small cabin. Cy Hungerford, a famed local political cartoonist of the 20th century, loved to retreat to this cozy one-room cabin to work on his newspaper cartoons in the peace of the woods. It's still known today as the Hungerford cabin and is sometimes used for educational programming.

Continuing on, you'll meander through oak and hickory forests using small bridges and boardwalks to cross over swampy areas. In the fall, the undergrowth is flush with purple asters and goldenrod. In the

springtime, areas along the Jennings Trail fill with vernal pools. These ephemeral pools appear in the spring from winter runoff and provide a habitat for amphibians. While walking in the evening, the woods will be filled with the high-pitched squeaks of spring peepers: tiny frogs no larger than your thumbnail!

After about a mile, you'll get on the green-blazed Meadow Trail to reach Raccoon Creek. This section of the reserve is flat and the undergrowth is teeming with Virginia Bluebells at the end of April. After a brief stint on the Hickory Trail, there's an easy spot to go out onto the creek bed and skip some stones or take in the soaring sycamore trees that line the creek. Continuing on the Hickory Trail to rejoin the Jennings Trail, you'll find the largest concentration of wildflower varieties. Just a few that you may see are red and white trilliums, yellow trout lilies, and the dainty Dutchman's Breeches. Many of these wildflowers are small and delicate, so it's especially important to stay on the trail and never pick any blooms.

After leaving the main section of wildflowers, you'll round a bend in the trail and head up the Max Henrici Trail, which ascends a gully to get back up the hill. At the top of the hill, you'll cross the road and then get on the yellow-marked Art Witt Trail as it heads into the pine trees and leads back to the parking lot.

## TURN-BY-TURN DIRECTIONS

1. Begin the hike at the covered kiosk with photos of the types of flowers and wildlife seen at the Reserve. Head into the woods on the Jennings Trail, marked with blue.
2. At 0.1 miles, pass the historic Hungerford Cabin. Follow the trail through the small field surrounding the cabin, then head back into the woods on the Jennings Trail.
3. At 0.2 miles, continue straight at the trail junction, remaining on the Jennings Trail.
4. At 0.7 miles, turn left to stay on the Jennings Trail, ignoring the spur trail to the right.
5. At 0.8 miles, turn right at the Y-junction onto the green-marked Meadow Trail.
6. At 0.9 miles, continue straight onto the pink-marked Hickory Trail. In 200 ft, take the unmarked side trail down to the creek bed. Then return to the Hickory Trail and continue.
7. At 1.1 miles, turn right at the T-junction onto the Meadow Trail.
8. At 1.2 miles, turn right to rejoin the blue-blazed Jennings Trail; this is the section of trail with the highest concentration of wildflowers.
9. At 1.6 miles, enjoy a view of the creek, then turn left onto the red-marked Max Henrici Trail heading uphill.
10. At 1.8 miles, continue straight at the four-way trail junction.
11. At 2.2 miles, carefully cross the road and continue into the woods, now on the yellow-marked Art Witt Trail. Finally, the Art Witt Trail meets up with the Jennings Trail and the kiosk from Step 1 is 100 feet to the left.

## FIND THE TRAILHEAD

From Pittsburgh, take I-376 W toward the Pittsburgh International Airport. Continue for 17.5 miles along the highway; then take Exit 52 for Clinton Road. At the end of the ramp, turn left at the stop sign onto Clinton Road. In 1.1 miles, turn right onto US-30 W. After 4.7 miles, turn right into the wildflower reserve. There is a small wooden sign designating the entrance. Proceed down the paved road for 200 feet and the gravel parking lot will be on the right. The trail begins at the far end of the parking lot by the wooden interpretive sign kiosk.

# FERMATA BREWING COMPANY

After years of homebrewing together, the pandemic left friends Chris Bendick, Alan Gore, Rob Smoker, and Jared Tuk with a lot of time to perfect their craft. The four friends dreamed of opening a cozy brewery embedded in a small town that could serve both as a craft beer venue and a gathering place for the community. As luck would have it, a 100-year-old former duckpin bowling alley on Merchant Street in Ambridge came up for lease at exactly the right time. The friends like to joke that they didn't choose Ambridge, Ambridge chose them.

These four friends are as passionate about music as they are craft beer, so this quickly became a guiding theme for their business. In written music, a fermata is a "pause of unspecified length over a note or rest." This is fitting because the brewery invites everyone to pause and stay for a while, enjoying live music with a beer in hand. Jared Tuk, a musician himself, books a variety of music acts at the taproom. They've featured everything from budding musicians to all-vinyl DJs.

Alan Gore, the head brewer, draws his recipes from a formative trip to Bavaria where he learned about traditional styles. However, he isn't afraid to experiment with big flavors either. The Cold Brew Collusion is an interesting combination of a crisp wheat beer brewed with the House Blend Coffee beans from their next-door neighbor Merchant Coffee Co. The unexpected combo of roasty coffee and crisp doughiness of the wheat beer pairs perfectly with your favorite cover band.

## LAND MANAGER

**PA Department of Conservation and Natural Resources**
3000 State Route 18
Hookstown, PA 15050-1605
(724) 899-2200
www.dcnr.pa.gov/StateParks/FindAPark/RaccoonCreekStatePark/
Map: elibrary.dcnr.pa.gov/GetDocument?docId=1742797&DocName=RACR_WildflowerReserveMap.pdf

## BREWERY/RESTAURANT

**Fermata Brewing Company**
918 Merchant Street
Ambridge, PA 15003
(724) 318-8189
www.fermatabrewing.beer

Distance from trailhead: 13 miles

# SLIPPERY ROCK GORGE

## A GORGE-OUS SCRAMBLE TO A COVERED BRIDGE AND GRISTMILL

| STARTING POINT | DESTINATION |
|---|---|
| HELL'S HOLLOW TRAILHEAD | MCCONNELLS MILL |
| **BREWERY** | **HIKE TYPE** |
| SHUBREW | STRENUOUS |
| **DOG-FRIENDLY** | **SEASON** |
| YES (LEASH REQUIRED) | YEAR-ROUND |
| **FEES** | **DURATION** |
| NO | 6 HOURS 30 MIN. |
| **MAP REFERENCE** | **LENGTH** |
| POSTED AT TRAILHEAD | 14.2 MILES (ROUND-TRIP) |
| **HIGHLIGHTS** | **ELEVATION GAIN** |
| HISTORIC COVERED BRIDGE, HIDDEN WATERFALLS | 1,430 FEET |

7.5 %
ALCOHOL CONTENT

## JUNGLEBOOT IPA

GOLDEN YELLOW

FLORAL

BITTERSWEET, CITRUS

BITTERNESS

SWEETNESS

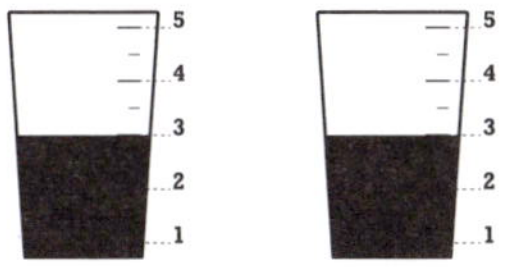


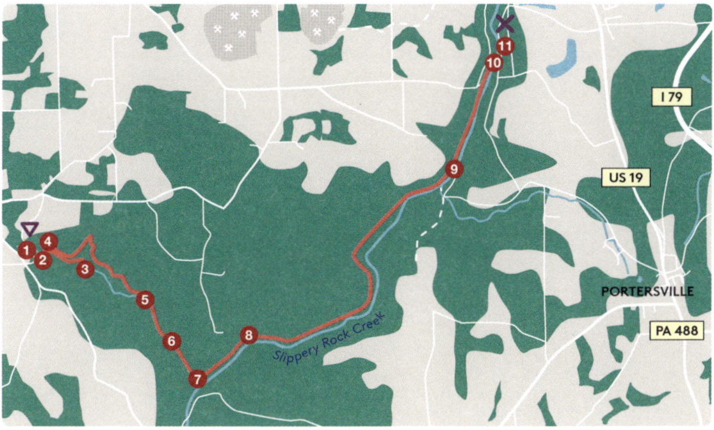


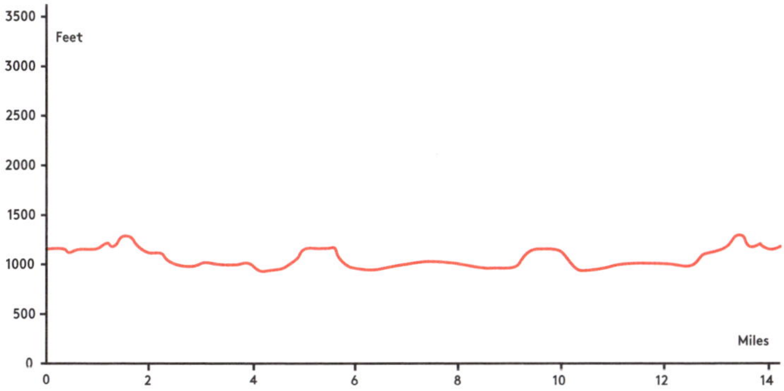

# HIKE DESCRIPTION

**Hike through an ancient gorge carved by glacial runoff to a historical covered bridge and gristmill. After this challenging but rewarding hike, treat yourself to a pint on the rooftop bar at Shubrew on the bustling Main Street of Zelienople.**

McConnells Mill State Park in Portersville, PA comprises over 2,500 acres and contains the stunning Slippery Rock Creek Gorge, a National Natural Landmark. The rocky landscape around the gorge was formed thousands of years ago by glacial runoff, which left behind boulders and unique geological features such as hidden waterfalls, land bridges, and tiny caves.

You'll start this hike on the short Hell's Hollow Trail, a flat path that meanders along a babbling stream called Hell Run. After about half a mile, you'll reach a set of wooden stairs leading down to a beautiful waterfall. From the trail's name, you might be expecting a difficult trek to the falls, but its ominous-sounding title is actually a reference to the lime kiln that once stood on the site, the remains of which can still be seen today beside the stairway. Locals used to say that the flames from the kiln looked like the fires of hell, but today these woods are more heavenly than hellish. The stairs end in the stream but there are stones you can step on to get a better view of the falls. Do not attempt when icy or when waters are high!

After seeing the falls, you'll backtrack along the Hell's Hollow Trail until you reach an intersection with a signpost pointing to Eckert Bridge. From here, you'll follow the Slippery Rock Gorge Trail, which is also part of the 4,000+ mile North Country Trail. After approximately 2 miles following the Hell Run creek, you'll meet the larger Slippery

Rock Creek and descend to the creek bed lined with boulders and hemlock trees. From here, you'll climb up and down rocky steps along the creek, which varies between raging rapids and peaceful waters. Sturdy footwear is a must for navigating the steep rock formations, and trekking poles might be helpful.

At the turnaround point, you'll reach one of the most photographed places in the park: the quintessential covered bridge and historic gristmill. The McConnell's Gristmill was a roller mill, and one of the first of its kind in the fledgling U.S. During its heyday in the late 1800s, the gristmill used water-powered turbines to grind up various grains for the local community. Now, it's a small museum and a great place to take a short break. Be sure to stop on the far side of the mill for the best photo opportunity, capturing both the mill and the covered bridge. Once you've snapped your pictures, retrace your steps along the Gorge Trail back to the Hell's Hollow parking lot.

## TURN-BY-TURN DIRECTIONS

1. From the trailhead kiosk at the parking lot, follow the trail over a small bridge.
2. At 0.1 miles, reach an intersection with a signpost for Eckert Bridge. Turn right onto the Hell's Hollow Trail, the opposite direction from Eckert Bridge (You'll go towards Eckert Bridge in step 3).
3. At 0.5 miles, take the stairs on the left down to the waterfall, and then retrace your steps back to step 2.
4. At 0.9 miles, reach the intersection from step 2. Turn right towards the sign for Eckert Bridge and onto the Slippery Rock Gorge Trail, marked with blue blazes on trees.
5. At 2.1 miles, cross a natural landbridge.
6. At 2.5 miles, use stepping stones to cross a small stream .
7. At 3 miles, bear left to meet up with the Slippery Rock Creek. Continue following the blue blazes on trees.

8. At 3.5 miles, dip into a small gully and cross a stream. The stream spills over the rock ledge creating a hidden waterfall. You can see it by carefully climbing down the hillside.
9. At 6.5 miles, pass Eckert Bridge. Do not cross the bridge, stay on the blue-blazed Slippery Rock Gorge Trail.
10. At 7.4 miles, merge onto McConnells Mill Road. Pass through the covered bridge with caution; this is an active road.
11. At 7.5 miles, the historic gristmill is to the left. From there, return the way you came, back to the Hell's Hollow parking lot.

## FIND THE TRAILHEAD

From Cranberry, head north on I-79. Take Exit 96 for PA-488 towards Portersville. Turn left onto PA-488. At the first light, about a half mile from the highway exit, turn right on Route 19 (Perry Highway). In 0.2 miles, turn left on W. Portersville Road. After 2 miles, bear right to get on Moundsville Road; proceed for 2.5 miles. Cross a bridge over the Slippery Rock Creek, getting a first view of the Gorge. Just after the bridge, turn right onto Heinz Camp Road. Continue for 2 miles, then turn right onto Shaffer Road. In 0.2 miles, the gravel parking lot will be on the left with a sign for Hell's Hollow, McConnells Mill State Park.

# SHUBREW

Shubrew has been a staple of Zelienople's main street since it first opened in 2013. In addition to house-made brews, it offers a delicious menu of sandwiches and pizza with lots of vegetarian options. Shubrew has grown quite a bit since their humble beginnings. Now, the husband and wife team, Zachary and Erika Shumaker, operate a brewing facility in the nearby town of Harmony, allowing them to produce larger batches and free up space in their taproom for more seating. After outgrowing their previous location across the street, the Shumakers moved into a larger space with tables and bar seating and features a seasonal rooftop patio. Fans of the old location won't be disappointed though; it's now a Chinese fusion restaurant, a side project of the Shumakers to experiment with their love of Chinese cuisine! Called General Shu's, it also features a lineup of Shubrew drafts. Shubrew offers a wide variety of beers with something for every type of beer drinker. Jungleboot IPA is their flagship IPA, and this hoppy beer really packs a punch! If you need a break from beer, they also offer a wide selection of cocktails and wine. You might even find yourself trying something unexpected. Hey, "if the Shu fits, drink it!"

## LAND MANAGER

**PA Department of Natural Resources**
Moraine State Park
225 Pleasant Valley Road
Portersville, PA 16051-9650
(724) 368-8811
www.dcnr.pa.gov/StateParks/FindAPark/McConnellsMillStatePark
Map: elibrary.dcnr.pa.gov/GetDocument?docId=1737472&DocName=MCMI_ParkMap.pdf

## BREWERY/RESTAURANT

**Shubrew**
205 South Main Street
Zelienople, PA 16063
(724) 766-4426
www.shubrew.com

Distance from trailhead: 14.6 miles

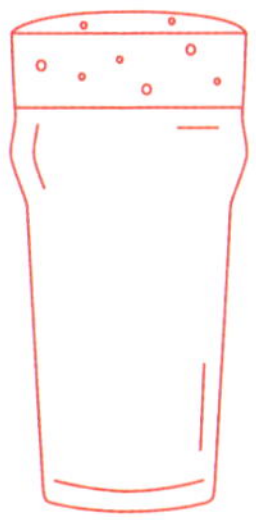

# GLACIER RIDGE TRAIL

## A PEACEFUL TREK THROUGH A FERN-FILLED FOREST TO A PICTURESQUE LAKE

| STARTING POINT | DESTINATION |
|---|---|
| GLACIER RIDGE TRAILHEAD | LAKE ARTHUR |
| BREWERY | HIKE TYPE |
| UNION BROTHER BREWING | MODERATE |
| DOG-FRIENDLY | SEASON |
| YES (LEASH REQUIRED) | YEAR-ROUND |
| FEES | DURATION |
| NO | 3 HOURS 30 MIN. |
| MAP REFERENCE | LENGTH |
| POSTED AT TRAILHEAD | 7.3 MILES (ROUND TRIP) |
| HIGHLIGHTS | ELEVATION GAIN |
| LAKESIDE, GLACIAL BOULDERS | 1,400 FEET |

4.7 %
ALCOHOL CONTENT

**SHORT BREAK SMALL HAZY IPA**

CLOUDY ORANGE

SWEET

LIGHT,
TANGY

BITTERNESS

SWEETNESS

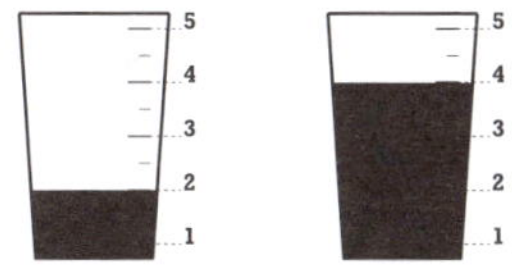


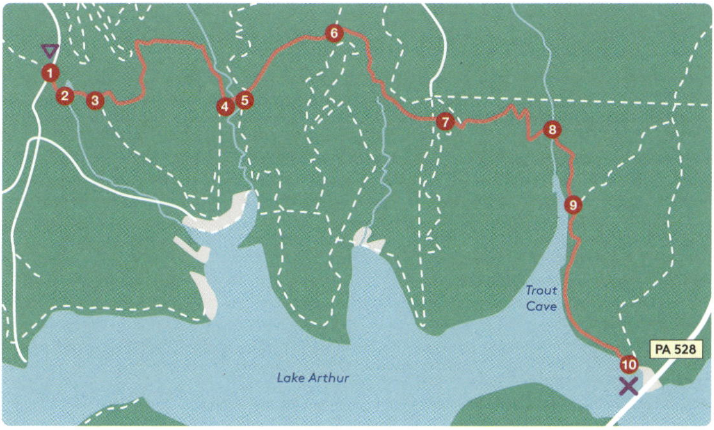


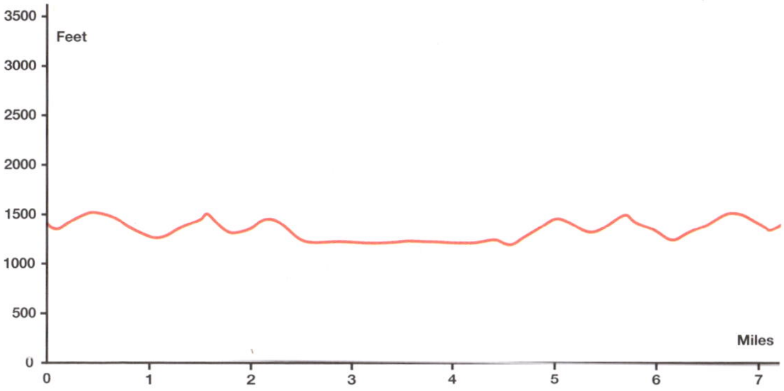

# HIKE DESCRIPTION

**Travel among diverse wildlife and rocky relics of the last ice age to the 3,225-acre Lake Arthur. Afterward, grab a bite to eat and sit back with a refreshing brew at the beer garden at Union Brothers Brewing.**

Moraine State Park is one of the largest parks in Western Pennsylvania, clocking over 16,725 acres and boasting over one million visitors per year to enjoy its lake and water recreation. However, it's easy to find solitude among its more than 28 miles of hiking, biking, and equestrian trails. The longest hike in the park is the Glacier Ridge Trail, which is a small slice of the North Country National Scenic Trail. While the full scenic trail is popular with backpackers, day hikers can tackle smaller sections like the Glacier Ridge Trail.

While passing through the lush woodland full of tulip poplars and ferns, keep an eye out along the trail for massive, lichen-covered boulders scattered throughout the landscape. Continental glaciers once covered about 30% of Pennsylvania and as these giant ice sheets ebbed away, masses of rock and sediment known as moraines were left behind, which is where this park gets its name. While passing these boulders in the shade of the trees, consider that this forest teeming with life was once a bleak landscape crushed under towering sheets of ice.

The Glacier Ridge Trail traces what was once the southernmost extent of the glacier. After passing a small pond just a few hundred yards from the trailhead, the trail climbs up and down the wooded, yet hilly landscape of the park. Descending closer to the water leads you out of the

dense woods and into marshy wetlands. Moraine State Park is probably best known for the large Lake Arthur at its center, which you'll reach approximately 3 miles into your hike. This lake was man-made when Frank W. Preston and the Western Pennsylvania Conservancy dammed a local creek to recreate the glacial lake that once existed in the area. Today, the lake is open for fishing, boating, swimming, and more. I highly suggest taking a swim in Lake Arthur after this hike!

## TURN-BY-TURN DIRECTIONS

1. From the parking lot, look for a small sign and map for the Glacial Ridge Trail and follow the blue blazes on signposts.
2. At 0.1 miles, pass a small pond on the left of the trail.
3. At 0.2 miles, at an intersection with a sign for the marina, continue straight to stay on the blue-blazed North Country Trail/Glacier Ridge Trail.
4. At 1.1 miles, bear left to stay on the blue-blazed trail, ignoring the trail with signs pointing to the marina.

5. At 1.2 miles, cross the bike path. Look out for mountain bikers!
6. At 1.6 miles, cross another bike path, continuing on the blue-blazed trail.
7. At 2.1 miles, reach an intersection with a red-blazed trail; continue straight to stay on the blue-blazed trail. In 100 feet, follow a sharp U-bend in the trail to stay on the blue-blazed trail.
8. At 2.6 miles, cross a bridge over a small stream intersecting the trail.
9. At 3.0 miles, reach a fork in the trail; ignore the North Country Trail on the left and continue straight on the white-blazed Glacier Ridge Trail, following the sign for the 528 bridge. This section of the trail hugs the lake shore and offers several spots to view the water.
10. At 4.1 miles, meet up with the 528 bridge parking lot and fishing pier. Turn around and retrace your steps back to the parking lot.

## FIND THE TRAILHEAD

From I-79 in Portersville, take Exit 99 for US-422. Continue for 0.4 miles, then take the exit for Park Street. After 500 feet, turn right at the stop sign onto W. Park Road; proceed for 2 miles. There will be many signs for Moraine State Park, but don't turn yet. After 2 miles, turn right onto Cornelius Road. Continue straight for 2 miles until the road turns into Mt. Union Road. After a mile, pass a large parking lot for the Moraine State Park bike trails; a few hundred feet further down the road, you'll find a gravel pull off for about 5 cars on the left side of the road. Park here and the trailhead and posted map will be to the right of the pull-off.

## BREWERY NAME AND DESCRIPTION

Union Brothers Brewing is a fairly recent addition to the thriving Butler County beer scene. Friends Zachary Waltz and Jeremiah Cain began homebrewing together and perfected their craft for many years before opening a taproom. Once they did, the demand for their lineup of sours and hazy IPAs quickly outgrew their first location.

The team has already expanded once to a larger taproom and in early 2024, they moved operations just down the street to a former Moose Fraternity Lodge building. From the stunning wall art by local graffiti artist Max Gonzales to its location down the street from the Steamfitters Union, Union Brothers is a celebration of the region's industrial past and present. Both brewers are proud members of their local union, which is how the brewery got its name. Whether in the hip taproom or sitting around picnic tables and fire pits outside, you'll find yourself right at home at Union Brothers. A full food menu caps Union Brothers off as the perfect place to unwind.

The Short Break Small IPA is a refreshingly hazy pour without the heaviness or high alcohol content of a typical NEIPA. Just like your union-mandated lunch break, Short Break is gone too quick!

### LAND MANAGER

**PA Department of Natural Resources**
℅ Moraine State Park
225 Pleasant Valley Road
Portersville, PA 16051-9650
(724) 368-8811
www.dcnr.pa.gov/StateParks/FindAPark/MoraineStatePark
Map: elibrary.dcnr.pa.gov/GetDocument?docId=1753227&DocName=MORA'_ParkMap.pdf

### BREWERY/RESTAURANT

**Union Brothers Brewing**
270 Mercer Street
Harmony, PA 16037
(724) 473-0964
www.unionbrothersbrewing.com

Distance from trailhead: 18 miles

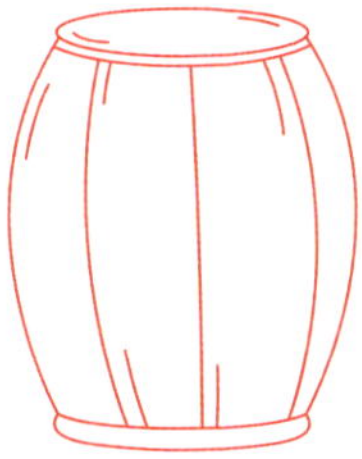

# FERNCLIFF PENINSULA

## HIKE TO A GRAND WATERFALL

| STARTING POINT | DESTINATION |
| --- | --- |
| GREAT ALLEGHENY PASSAGE PARKING LOT | OHIOPYLE FALLS |
| BREWERY | HIKE TYPE |
| YOUGH RIVER BREWING CO. | MODERATE |
| DOG-FRIENDLY | SEASON |
| YES (LEASH REQUIRED) | YEAR-ROUND |
| FEES | DURATION |
| NONE | 1 HOUR |
| MAP REFERENCE | LENGTH |
| ALLTRAILS | 1.8 MILES (LOOP) |
| HIGHLIGHTS | ELEVATION GAIN |
| WATERFALL, RIVER, ROCK SCRAMBLES | 164 FEET |

**6.4%** ALCOHOL CONTENT

## BEARDED NOMAD NEW ENGLAND IPA

LIGHT ORANGE

HOPPY, TROPICAL

SWEETLY CITRUS

BITTERNESS

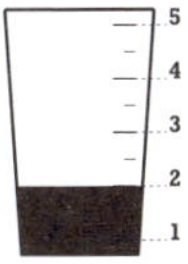


SWEETNESS

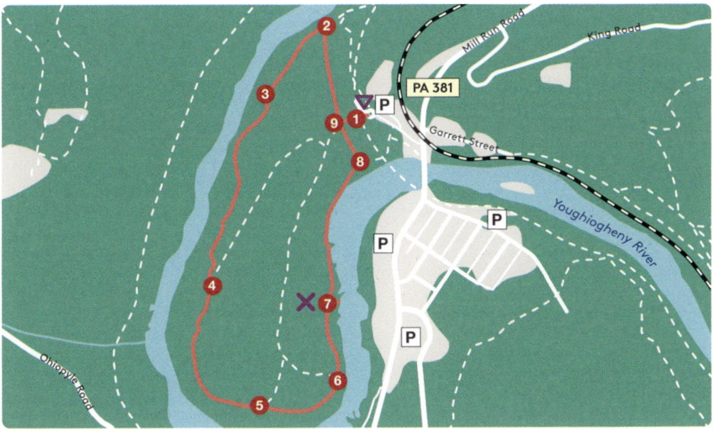


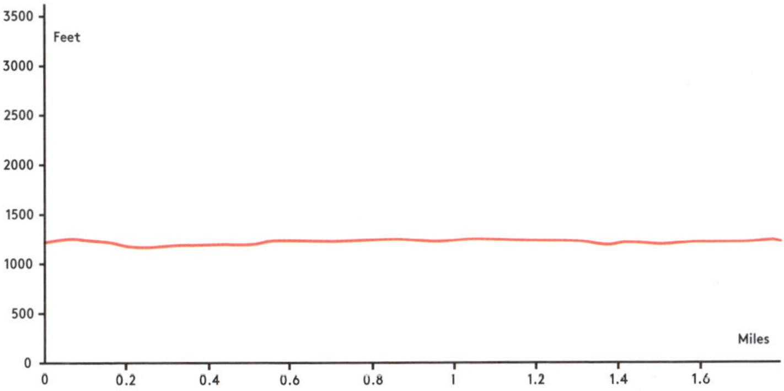

# HIKE DESCRIPTION

**Take this short but rewarding loop through an old-growth forest to see the roaring Ohiopyle Falls. Finish your day at Yough River Brewing Co. for tasty brews around outdoor fire pits.**

Ohiopyle State Park is a gem of the Laurel Highlands region of Southwestern Pennsylvania and is a popular day trip from Pittsburgh. While there are over 83 miles of trail in the park, this short loop offers a mouth-watering taste of the region's beauty, exploring a specific part called the Ferncliff Natural Area. Following the Ferncliff Trail allows a full loop along the edge of the peninsula overlooking the Youghiogheny River.

From the parking lot, you'll find a plaque designating the Ferncliff Peninsula as a Natural Landmark. In the late 1800s, industry brought more people to the region and the town of Ohiopyle quickly became popular with tourists. It's hard to believe while walking through the towering trees, but the peninsula was once home to the Ferncliff Hotel, a fashionable destination for the wealthier families of Pittsburgh. Eventually, the rise of automobiles led to the decline of resorts

like these and the Ferncliff hotel was torn down in 1940. The Kaufman family (of department store fame) frequented the Southwest Pennsylvania area to stay at their home, called Fallingwater, which was designed by Frank Lloyd Wright. Edgar Kaufman loved the surrounding landscape and eventually purchased the Ferncliff Peninsula, in addition to many acres surrounding Fallingwater. He gifted the land to the Western Pennsylvania Conservancy, and in the mid-1960s, it was incorporated into Ohiopyle State Park.

The initial first miles of the hike are a pleasant walk through tall hemlock trees with chances to see 300-million-year-old fossils in the exposed sandstone rock. Keep your eyes peeled; they will look like bike tracks embedded in the stone! Through gaps in the trees, you'll spy the white-watered river below as it crashes over the rocks. Ohiopyle is a world-class rafting destination and the Class III and IV rapids around the peninsula make for an exciting challenge for experienced rafters. In fact, the rapids are such a trademark of the area that the name "Ohiopyle" comes from a native Lenape word meaning "to turn white," in reference to the foamy water as it cascades over the rocks.

After rounding the tip of the peninsula, you'll follow the trail through a tunnel of green, surrounded by dense rhododendron thickets. Just over a mile in, you'll find a set of wooden steps on the right leading out to a viewpoint of the mighty Ohiopyle Falls that span the breadth of the river. This is a majestic spot, so take lots of pictures and enjoy yourself! Across the way is the visitor's center with a floor-to-ceiling glass room for viewing the falls. A visit is highly recommended after your hike.

After the vista, the trail leaves the woods and heads out along the riverside rocks. Be careful during rainy times and be aware that during heavy rainfall this trail section could be underwater. When the rocks aren't covered by water, this is an incredible spot to experience the great river up close. When you've taken in all the sights and sounds, continue along the trail, following along the river's edge. The trail eventually bears to the left to take the Ferncliff trail back to the trailhead.

## TURN-BY-TURN DIRECTIONS

1. From the parking lot, head into the woods on the trail marked by yellow blazes on trees. Cross over the wide gravel bike path and then turn right at the trail intersection marked by a large rock with a metal plaque for the Ferncliff Peninsula Natural Area.
2. At 0.2 miles, turn left to stay on the Ferncliff Trail.
3. At 0.3 miles, reach a break in the trees for a rocky view of the river below.
4. At 0.7 miles, at the Y-junction, stay right on the Ferncliff Trail.
5. At 1.0 miles, continue straight at the trail junction, ignoring the trail to the left.
6. At 1.2 miles, at the Y-junction, stay right to stay on the Ferncliff Trail.
7. At 1.3 miles, take the wooden stairs on the right to walk down to the rock outcropping for a view of Ohiopyle Falls. Return up the stairs and then turn right.
8. At 1.6 miles, turn left onto the Ferncliff Trail.
9. At 1.7 miles, return to the intersection from Step 1. Turn right to return to the parking lot and complete the loop.

# FIND THE TRAILHEAD

From Pittsburgh, follow Route 51 south. After 42 miles, take the right exit lane to merge onto US-119 S. Proceed for 1.5 miles and then stay in the leftmost lane to stay on US-119/US-40. After 2.3 miles, stay in the left-most lane again to stay on US-40 as it splits from US-119. After 8 miles, turn left at the traffic light onto Chalk-Hill-Ohiopyle Road. After 3.2 miles, the road turns into Kentuck Road. After 3.5 miles, turn right at the stop sign, following the sign for the Park Office. Follow the winding road for 1.5 miles before turning left at the stop sign onto Main Street. Proceed for 0.6 miles, passing the Park Office on the left and continuing under the underpass. Immediately after the underpass the parking lot for the Ferncliff Natural Area will be on the left marked by a brown arrow pointing to the gravel parking area. If the Ferncliff parking area is full, you can park at the larger park office parking lot and walk to the trailhead.

# YOUGH RIVER BREWING CO.

The idea for Yough River Brewing started as many great ideas do: over a cold beer. While seeing the crowd of patrons at a bustling brewery, Matt Humes had the grand idea to open a brewery near his hometown of Connellsville. He and his wife Jacquelyn were born and raised in the small town and always felt that its proximity to the Laurel Highlands and the Great Allegheny Passage (GAP) bike trail made it ideal as a craft beverage destination. What Matt may have lacked in experience, he made up for in gumption!

He immediately started homebrewing and within a year, had taken steps to make his brewery dream a reality. However, starting a brewery while working full-time had its difficulties; Matt recalls the brutal days of trying to get the brewery up and running while juggling his full-time job as a bricklayer. Thankfully, those skills came in handy when Matt decided to save money on the brewery by converting his equipment storage building into a taproom. The location offers plenty of parking, and its location right on the GAP trail and Youghiogheny River can't be beat. Matt also brought on a professional brewer to help make the leap from homebrew to commercial brewing. Yough River Brewing officially opened in April 2022 and was welcomed with open arms as the first taproom in Fayette County. Their flagship hazy IPA, the Bearded Nomad, is a must for fans of a perfectly balanced hop and fruit combo.

## LAND MANAGER

**PA Department of Natural Resources**
124 Main Street
Ohiopyle, PA 15470
724-329-8591
www.dcnr.pa.gov/StateParks/FindAPark/OhiopyleStatePark
Map: elibrary.dcnr.pa.gov/GetDocument?docId=1737407&DocName=OHIO_ParkMap.pdf

## BREWERY/RESTAURANT

**Yough River Brewing Co.**
1030 South Arch Street
Connellsville, PA 15425
(724) 322-4568
www.youghriverbrewing.com

Distance from trailhead: 19 miles

# ADAM FALLS AND FLAT ROCK

## A PICTURESQUE WATERFALL IN THE HEART OF THE LAUREL HIGHLANDS

| STARTING POINT | DESTINATION |
|---|---|
| ADAM FALLS PICNIC AREA | ADAM FALLS |
| **BREWERY** | **HIKE TYPE** |
| UNITY BREWING | MODERATE |
| **DOG-FRIENDLY** | **SEASON** |
| YES (LEASH REQUIRED) | YEAR-ROUND |
| **FEES** | **DURATION** |
| NONE | 1 HOUR |
| **MAP REFERENCE** | **LENGTH** |
| POSTED AT TRAILHEAD | 2.2 MILES (LOOP) |
| **HIGHLIGHTS** | **ELEVATION GAIN** |
| HISTORIC RUINS, STREAMSIDE, PICNIC AREA | 266 FEET |

**5.0%**
ALCOHOL CONTENT

# MIDWAY CABIN VANILLA PORTER

DEEP BLACK

VANILLA COFFEE

SMOOTH COCOA

**BITTERNESS**

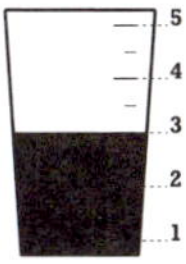


**SWEETNESS**

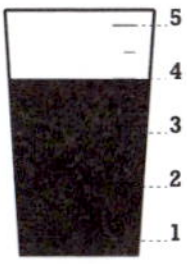


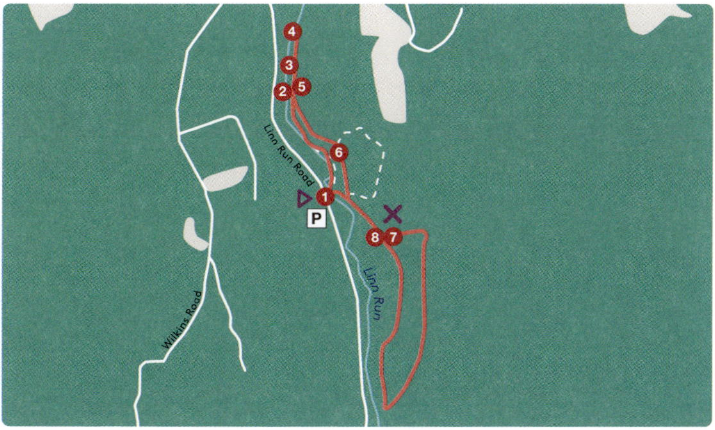


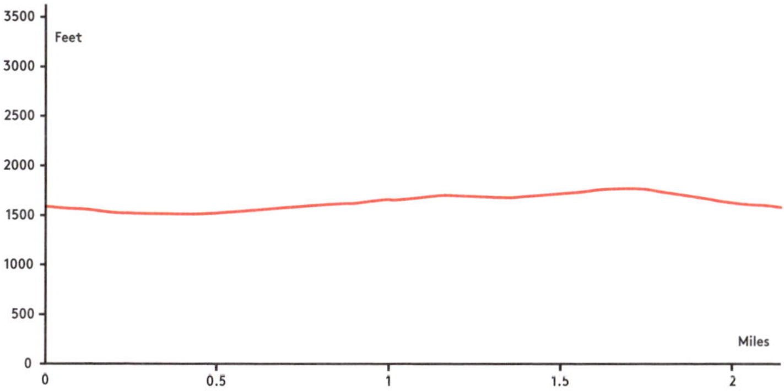

# HIKE DESCRIPTION

**Hike through peaceful woods in the Laurel Highlands to a small waterfall along the charming Linn Run. Afterward, feel like a part of the commUnity at Unity Brewing taproom and restaurant.**

Linn Run State Park is one of the eight state parks that make up the Laurel Highlands region. Although one of the smaller parks, Linn Run has hiking trails, cabins, fishing, and picnicking. Plus, many of the trails connect to the 50,000-acre Forbes State Forest that surrounds it. This scenic park is the perfect summer getaway for the whole family. The short hike combines two of the most popular hikes: the Adam Falls and Flat Rock Trails.

You'll start at the parking lot for Adam Falls Picnic Area. Here, you'll find picnic tables and charcoal grills, perfect for a post-hike cookout (If this lot is full, there's overflow parking in the grass across the street or in the upper parking lot up the gravel road further into the park). Linn Run is a popular local spot so you'll likely be sharing the trails with other hiking enthusiasts, especially during the summer.

First up, you'll tackle the Flat Rock Trail, a wide path that winds along the shallow waters of Linn Run. Thick patches of mountain laurel, Pennsylvania's state flower, line the streambed and explode in hues of white and pink in late May. Small picturesque cabins sit across the water and you may spot fishermen patiently waiting to hook a trout in the stream. As you walk along the peaceful waters under the shade of tall hardwood and hemlock trees, it's difficult to imagine that when the state purchased this land in 1909, it was completely clear-cut by the logging industry. The damage was so devastating that the government had to import deer back into the area during revitalization efforts. Thankfully, Linn Run has undergone a complete transformation since those dark days. Now, it's a flourishing second-growth forest.

After a quarter mile along the trail, you'll come across the ruins of a stone building; this was once an old hunting lodge, but a fire destroyed it in the 1940s. These ruins are fascinating to explore, especially the completely intact towering chimney. From here, it's about a quarter mile more until you reach Flat Rock. True to its name, Flat Rock is a very shallow section of Linn Run where a large flat rock creates a smooth cascade of water. Although many use this as a natural water slide, note that the park prohibits swimming. The view is best enjoyed safely from the banks. From Flat Rock, you'll retrace your steps past the hunting lodge ruins and follow the brown and yellow signs for Adam Falls. You'll walk through the upper parking lot, an alternate parking location if the main lot is full. Just past the gravel access road to the parking lot, the trail leads back into the woods and to a quaint wooden bridge. This places you directly on top of the 15-foot Adam Falls. Another 100 feet and you'll reach the final destination of this trail where you'll enjoy an overlook with a perfect view of the petite falls. The view is especially scenic after a rainfall when the water flow is heaviest.

The rest of the hike is a pleasant, one-mile loop through the woods. You'll encounter a few minor rocky spots and pass alongside huge lichen-covered boulders. The Adam Falls Trail ends at the bridge to the waterfall, where you'll finish the route by heading down the gravel road back to the Adam Falls Picnic Area parking lot.

## TURN-BY-TURN DIRECTIONS

1. From the Adam Falls Picnic Area parking lot, cross the gravel access road to the picnic area. Follow the sign for the Flat Rock Trail to start on the wide path along the waterside marked by yellow blazes.
2. At 0.2 miles, at the junction, stay straight on the Flat Rock Trail.
3. At 0.3 miles, walk past stone ruins to the left. After exploring the ruins, continue along the trail.
4. At 0.4 miles, reach the flat rock water feature in the stream where the trail ends. Retrace your steps along the Flat Rock Trail back toward the ruins.
5. At 0.6 miles, return to the trail intersection from Step 2 and take the left trail to get on the Adam Falls Trail.
6. At 0.8 miles, pass through the gravel upper parking lot. At the end of the parking lot, follow the trail signs for Adam Falls back onto the dirt path.
7. At 1.0 miles, turn right to cross the wooden bridge that spans the small stream. The waterfall is directly below. After 100 feet more, there is a wide view of the falls. Continue along the Adam Fall Trail loop.
8. At 2.1 miles, complete the Adam Falls Trail loop. Continue straight on the gravel road leading back down to the parking lot.

## FIND THE TRAILHEAD

From Latrobe, follow Route 30 (The Lincoln Highway) heading east for 9 miles. At a traffic light in Ligonier, turn right onto S. Market Street/ PA 711 S. Continue for 3.5 miles, then turn left onto Darlington Rector Road. After 1 mile, turn right onto Linn Run Road, which leads into the park. In 2 miles, the parking area is on the left marked by a brown sign for Adam Falls Picnic Area. The trail begins in the picnic area to the left of the gravel parking lot.

# UNITY BREWING

Kevin Ridilla had been homebrewing for nearly 2 decades when a close friend finally flat-out asked if he was ever going to open his own place. As the co-owner of a flooring business with his wife Kristy, Kevin had toyed with the idea of opening a taproom for years but had never acted on it. Suddenly, it seemed like it was finally time to make that dream a reality. After securing a location, DIY-ing renovations, and bringing on a friend to help with brewing operations, Unity Brewing was all set to open. They were open for nine whole days in March 2020 before the pandemic changed everything. Through perseverance and the endless support of the Latrobe community, Unity Brewing now stands as a staple of the town.

When searching for a name for his fledgling brewery, Kevin knew that Unity was the perfect fit. Not only is it the name of the township where the Latrobe taproom is situated, but it also completely encapsulates the mission of the brewery. When you walk into the colorful taproom, filled with vibrant local art, you immediately become part of the Unity family.

Although now employing a full-time brewer, Kevin still likes to experiment with flavors when not managing the taproom and kitchen. One of his creative flavor pairings from the early days, the Vanilla Bean Blonde Ale is a long-standing crowd favorite of the pub. Another vanilla favorite, the featured Vanilla Porter Midway Cabin is a warming homage to the skiing culture of the Laurel Highlands; it's named for the original ski lodge at Laurel Mountain.

## LAND MANAGER

**PA Department of Natural Resources**
770 Linn Run Road
Rector, PA 15677
(724) 238-6623
www.dcnr.pa.gov/StateParks/FindAPark/LinnRunStatePark
Map: elibrary.dcnr.pa.gov/GetDocument?docId=1737528&Doc-Name=LIRU_ParkMap.pdf

## BREWERY/RESTAURANT

**Unity Brewing**
3862 US-30,
Latrobe, PA 15650
(724) 520-4234
www.unitybrewingpa.com

Distance from trailhead: 16 miles

# PRESQUE ISLE STATE PARK

## HIKE ALONG THE BEACHES OF PRESQUE ISLE

| STARTING POINT | DESTINATION |
|---|---|
| PARKING LOT FOR BEACH #10 | GULL POINT VIEWING PLATFORM |
| **BREWERY** | **HIKE TYPE** |
| ERIE BREWING CO. | EASY |
| **DOG-FRIENDLY** | **SEASON** |
| YES (LEASH REQUIRED) | APRIL–OCTOBER |
| **FEES** | **DURATION** |
| NONE | 1 HOUR 20 MIN. |
| **MAP REFERENCE** | **LENGTH** |
| ALLTRAILS | 3.1 MILES (ROUND TRIP) |
| **HIGHLIGHTS** | **ELEVATION GAIN** |
| BEACH, BIRDWATCHING | 15 FEET |

6.5 % ALCOHOL CONTENT

## JOHNNY RAILS PUMPKIN ALE

COPPER

WARM SPICES

SWEET MALTY

BITTERNESS

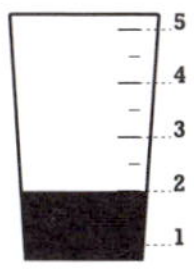


SWEETNESS

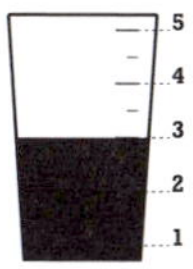


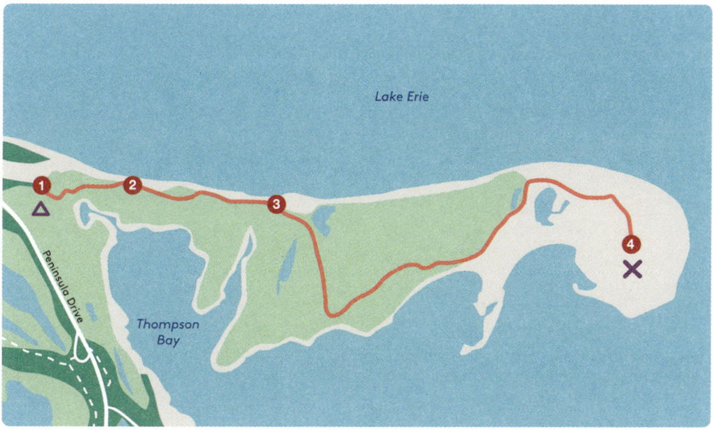


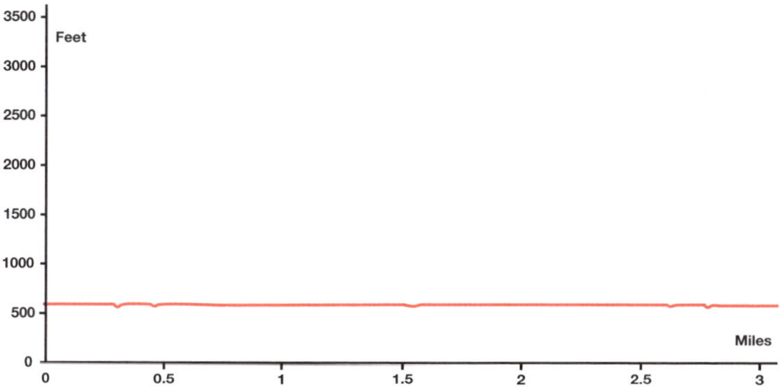

# HIKE DESCRIPTION

**Hike along Pennsylvania's only "seashore" hugging the waters of Lake Erie to a birdwatcher's paradise. Afterward, head to the mainland for a pint at Erie Brewing Co.'s spacious West Side taproom in an old dance hall.**

Located on a sandy peninsula that arcs into Lake Erie, Presque Isle State Park is the most-visited state park in Pennsylvania. Lake Erie offers visitors a taste of beach life while in a land-locked state. Although the waters aren't salty, the 241-mile-long lake is vast enough to seem like a calm ocean when peering into the hazy distance. They're called "Great" lakes for a reason!

The Great Lakes Region has a fascinating geological history. Scientists believe that the whole of Lake Erie was once a massive ice cap. At the end of the last ice age, glaciers receded and melted, filling a large

valley to create Lake Erie. The receding glaciers also left behind deposits of rock and sediment which eventually formed the peninsula. This narrow, sandy expanse juts 4 miles into the lake, forming a bay between the City of Erie and the lake. Now preserved as a state park, the park features 10 beaches, 21 miles of trails (paved and unpaved), and a boating marina.

Before starting out a visit to the park, stop by the Tom Ridge Environmental Center just before entering the park. This educational facility offers exhibits, videos, and programs relating to Lake Erie's ecology, wildlife, history, and more.

This hike leads you to one of the most important birding spots in the park. Although popular for its recreational amenities, Presque Isle is also an incredible ecologically-diverse region. In fact, the park is a National Natural Landmark thanks to its popularity with migratory birds. Gull Point is so critical for migrating birds that the park closes the area from October 31 to April 1 for nesting birds. The ecosystem at Gull Point is incredibly fragile, so it's especially important to remain on designated trails. The first part of the trail begins in the grassy lowlands before quickly emerging onto the beach. There's no signage on this section, so just follow along the water's edge. Driftwood logs offer a perfect seat for taking in the lapping waters on the shore. Toward the end of the beach, bear right to follow the sandy trail into the tall grasses. From here, the trail meanders through grass and alongside marshy patches. It can get quite muddy and buggy in the sunny seasons, so plan accordingly. Finally, the trail emerges onto a broad sandy expanse with views of the City of Erie to the right and the open waters to the left. Ahead you'll see the observation tower—here, you'll be able to see the highest concentration of birds. Remember that spotting wildlife takes quiet and patience, so this is a good hike to slow down and spend some quiet time with nature.

## TURN-BY-TURN DIRECTIONS

1. From the parking lot, head toward the yellow trail marker for the Gull Point Trail at the southeast corner of the parking lot.
2. At 0.2 miles, emerge onto the beach and continue right along the water's edge.
3. At 0.5 miles, make a slight right to follow the trail into the grasses and through the marsh.
4. At 1.5 miles, reach the Gull Point Observation Tower. After taking in the views, turn around and return the way you came.

## FIND THE TRAILHEAD

From I-79N in Erie, take Exit 182 to merge onto US-20W/ W. 26th Street. Proceed for 0.7 miles, then turn right at the traffic light onto Peninsula Drive. After 1.6 miles, pass between the water park and the Tom Ridge Environmental Center to enter the park. Continue along Peninsula Drive for 4 miles through the park. At the stop sign, keep left to stay on Peninsula Drive. After 2 miles, find the parking lot for Beach 10 on the left. The trail begins at the yellow marker in the southeast corner of the lot.

# ERIE BREWING CO.

For over three decades, Erie Brewing Co. has been churning out kegs in Pennsylvania's fifth largest city. After that long, you learn a thing or two about making good beer! Things haven't always been easy, but a change in management in 2012 led to explosive growth for this once-modest brewing company.

From the early days of being the first microbrewery in Northeast Pennsylvania, Erie Brewing Co. now distributes to 13 states and operates two taprooms in Erie. With owner Rob Lowther at the helm, the main brewery is located outside of the city in Knowledge Park where they brew up favorites like Railbender IPA and the Bayshore Blonde Ale. However, demand from beer-lovers in the city led Lowther to look for a location closer to downtown. Fortuitous events led to the purchase of a historic building that was perfect for the kind of family-friendly, restaurant environment Lowther had in mind. Opening in 2020, the former Sportsman Club building has new life as a large taproom complete with indoor and outdoor fireplaces, a gift shop, and in-house restaurant partner Beechwood Inn's Hardwood Grille, which specializes in mouthwatering burgers. Whether pulling up to the bar or settling into a couch with a board game, there's a spot for everyone.

The seasonal favorite Johnny Rails Ale is sure to delight anyone who enjoys crisp mornings and firepit nights. Yes, it's a pumpkin beer, but the blonde ale base allows the melding of pumpkin and spices to settle lightly on the tongue. It's the perfect beer for a seasonal transition from beaches to falling leaves.

## LAND MANAGER

**PA Department of Natural Resources**
Presque Isle State Park
301 Peninsula Drive, Suite 1
Erie, PA 16505
(814) 833-7424
www.dcnr.pa.gov/StateParks/FindAPark/PresqueIsleStatePark
Map: elibrary.dcnr.pa.gov/GetDocument?docId=1737342&DocName=PRES_ParkMap.pdf

## BREWERY/RESTAURANT

**Erie Brewing Co. – West Side**
4102 West Lake Road
Erie, PA 16505
(814) 651-0611
www.eriebrewingco.com

Distance from trailhead: 8.2 miles

# FOREST CATHEDRAL

## ROAM THROUGH THE ANCIENTS IN COOK FOREST

| STARTING POINT | DESTINATION |
|---|---|
| LOG CABIN ENVIRONMENTAL CENTER | TOM'S RUN |

| BREWERY | HIKE TYPE |
|---|---|
| LOST IN THE WILDS BREWING | EASY |

| DOG-FRIENDLY | SEASON |
|---|---|
| YES (LEASH REQUIRED) | YEAR-ROUND |

| FEES | DURATION |
|---|---|
| NONE | 45 MIN. |

| MAP REFERENCE | LENGTH |
|---|---|
| ALLTRAILS | 1.6 MILES (LOOP) |

| HIGHLIGHTS | ELEVATION GAIN |
|---|---|
| OLD GROWTH FOREST, STREAM | 184 FEET |

6.2%
ALCOHOL CONTENT

## BEAR FOX BROWN ALE

COPPERY BROWN

SWEET AND MALTY

BROWN SUGAR, DRIED FRUIT

BITTERNESS

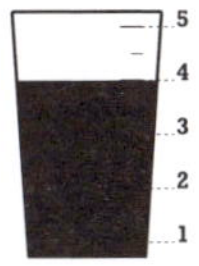


SWEETNESS

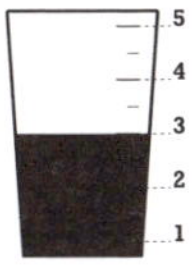


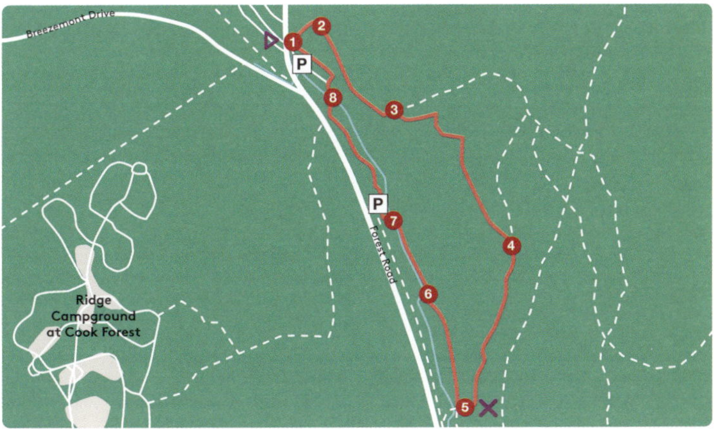


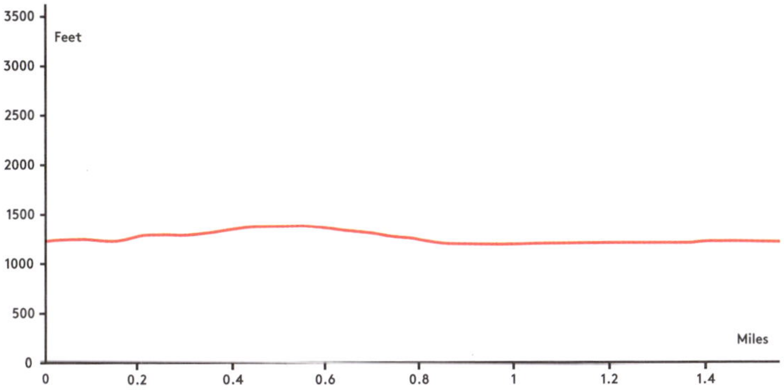

# HIKE DESCRIPTION

**Explore Pennsylvania's largest old-growth forest where 300-year-old trees tower overhead. Afterward, head to Lost in the Wilds Brewing where you can find yourself a cold brew tucked among the trees.**

Cook Forest State Park is nestled near the Allegheny National Forest in the northeastern corner of Pennsylvania. It's part of a greater region known as the Pennsylvania Wilds, whose 12 counties house only 4% of the state's population. This sparsely populated area offers some of the most stunning natural landscape the state has to offer.

The Forest Cathedral Area is Pennsylvania's largest old-growth forest and a registered National Natural Landmark. This short and easy hike takes you through an ancient forest of white pine and hemlock trees. Our hike starts on the Longfellow Trail, which begins to the right of the Log Cabin Environmental Center and is marked by a large wooden sign and blue and yellow blazes. The first part is also a section of the North Country Scenic Trail, a roughly 4,800-mile trail that stretches from North Dakota to Vermont and is always marked by light blue blazes.

You'll head up the hill on the Longfellow Trail where, in a few hundred feet, you'll see a sign for the "Tree of Peace." This white pine was planted by Mohawk Chief Jake Tekaronianeken Swamp who created the Tree of Peace Society in 1984 to advocate for peace and greater ecological awareness. Past the Tree of Peace on the left is a stone fountain emerging from the hillside. Built in 1950, this memorial commemorates the original members of the Cook Forest Association who raised the funds to purchase and preserve the state park land. While a beautiful tribute, note that the fountain water is not potable.

Continuing up the Longfellow Trail, the path is wide and towering evergreens surround you. Even in winter, their evergreen needles dapple the sunlight and create a soft, quiet underbrush. After rainy days and during the spring, you'll find runoff streams trickling down the hillside and over the moss-covered stones. The majesty of the enormous trees along the path is stunning, with some of these trees being nearly 350 years old. Only 1% of old-growth forests remain in the Eastern United States, and it's especially miraculous that a patch of old growth forest the size of the Forest Cathedral survived the logging boom of the late 1800s. However, it's humbling to see the number of fallen trunks as well, knowing that even these giants can succumb to heavy storms.

About a quarter of a mile into the hike, you'll leave the Longfellow Trail to get on the Ancient Forest Trail, marked by a brown post. This trail contains some of the largest remaining white pines in the park. Soft beds of moss and ferns line the underbrush of these massive trees. As

the trail meets back up with the Longfellow Trail, rhododendron and mountain laurel thickets emerge as you begin to descend the hillside. Leaving the old-growth area, you'll reach Tom's Run, a popular fishing spot. The Tom's Run Trail is an easy path that crosses over the stream several times using sturdy, wide bridges. After about a mile and a half, you'll pass a picnic shelter and follow along the gravel access road before passing over a final bridge that connects to the parking lot.

## TURN-BY-TURN DIRECTIONS

1. Starting at the large wooden sign in front of the log cabin, follow the blue and yellow marked Longfellow Trail into the woods on the right side of the cabin.
2. At 0.1 miles, pass the interpretive sign for the Tree of Peace. In 100 feet, pass the large stone Memorial Fountain.
3. At 0.3 miles, turn right at the Y-junction onto the Ancient Forest Trail, which is marked by a wooden signpost and yellow tree markings.
4. At 0.5 miles, rejoin the Longfellow Trail with its blue and yellow markings as the trail heads downhill.
5. At 0.9 miles, emerge onto a trail junction at a stream. Use the bridge to cross the stream and then continue to the right on the Tom's Run Trail, marked by a signpost and yellow markings.
6. At 1.1 miles, cross the next bridge over the stream, staying on the Tom's Run Trail.
7. At 1.2 miles, cross another bridge, then pass in front of a picnic pavilion. Follow the trail into the gravel parking lot and continue onto the park road.
8. At 1.4 miles, bear right, leaving the road and getting back onto the trail. Use the bridge to cross the stream a final time and then follow the trail back to the Log Cabin Environmental Center parking lot.

# FIND THE TRAILHEAD

From Clarion, get on State Route 1005 north and proceed for 11 miles. At a stop sign, turn right onto PA-36 South. After 3 miles, make a sharp left turn onto Forest Road. If you pass the State Park Office, you have gone too far on PA-36 South. After 1 mile on Forest Road, the parking lot will be on your right. There is a prominent wooden sign for the Log Cabin Environmental Center at the parking lot entrance.

## LOST IN THE WILDS BREWING

Lost in the Wilds Brewing is a haven for outdoor lovers. Husband and wife owners Jared and Mallory Griebel love the great outdoors and are passionate about sharing it with everyone, so their brewery is fittingly tucked into the woods. It has grown popular with tourists and locals alike and the couple loves sharing their favorite spots to escape into nature with anyone that pulls up a chair at the bar. While traveling together over the years, Jared and Mallory always found themselves drawn to the local craft brewery in the towns they visited, inspiring them to try homebrewing themselves. From brewing for a friend's wedding to medaling in homebrew competitions, they realized they had something special to share and decided to take a shot at opening a brewery like the ones that inspired them. After years of traveling, they were determined to move back to their hometown and build a brewery that would bring state park traffic to Shippenville. Despite opening in the midst of a global pandemic, the Griebels have stayed strong and have even expanded their taproom to include a large outdoor space for music and a secondary bar.

Bear Fox is a delicious brown ale with a slightly sweet brown sugar flavor balanced by a full, malty body. The ale is lovingly named for the Griebels' nicknames for their two dogs and is best enjoyed outside beneath the trees and with a furry friend if you have one handy.

### LAND MANAGER

**PA Department of Natural Resources**
100 Rt 36, P.O. Box 120
Cooksburg, PA 16217
(814) 744-8407
www.dcnr.pa.gov/StateParks/FindAPark/CookForestStatePark
Map: elibrary.dcnr.pa.gov/GetDocument?docId=1753274&DocName=COOK_TrailGuide.pdf

### BREWERY/RESTAURANT

**Lost in the Wilds Brewing**
21964 PA-66
Shippenville, PA 16254
(814) 227-8976
www.lostinthewildsbrewing.com

Distance from trailhead: 18 miles

# CENTRAL PENNSYLVANIA

# KINZUA BRIDGE

## HIKE THE FORMER TALLEST RAILROAD BRIDGE

| STARTING POINT | DESTINATION |
|---|---|
| KINZUA BRIDGE STATE PARK OFFICE | SKYWALK |
| BREWERY | HIKE TYPE |
| LOGYARD BREWING | MODERATE |
| DOG-FRIENDLY | SEASON |
| YES (LEASH REQUIRED) | YEAR-ROUND |
| FEES | DURATION |
| NONE | 1 HOUR |
| MAP REFERENCE | LENGTH |
| POSTED AT TRAILHEAD | 1.5 MILES (ROUND TRIP) |
| HIGHLIGHTS | ELEVATION GAIN |
| COLLAPSED VIADUCT, SKYWALK | 505 FEET |

**4.6%** ALCOHOL CONTENT

## GREENHORN SESSION IPA

LIGHT YELLOW

CITRUS

SMOOTH, HOPPY

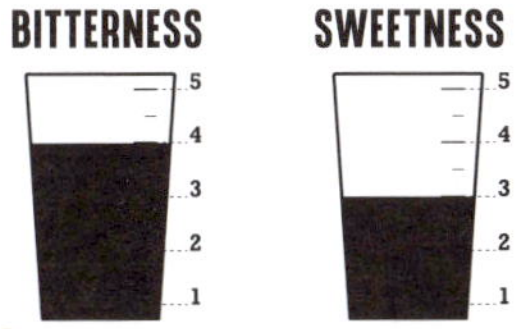


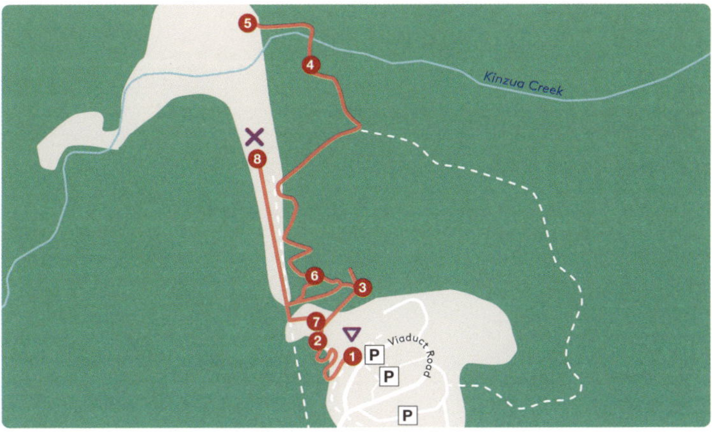


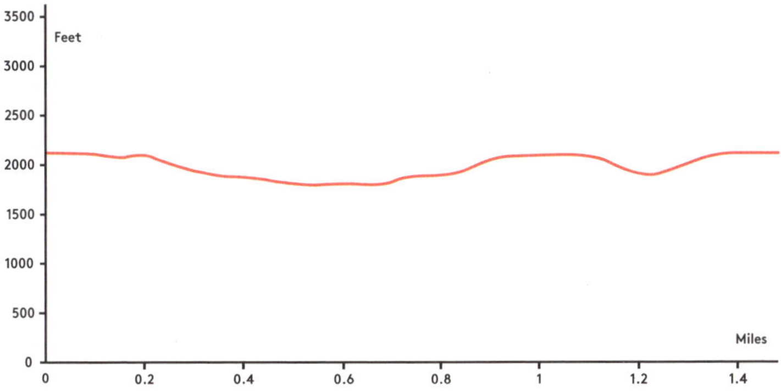

# HIKE DESCRIPTION

**Hike into the Kinzua Gorge to see the remains of the once-tallest railroad bridge in the world. Afterward, head to Logyard Brewing in the quaint town of Kane for a pint at a logging-themed taphouse.**

Since the 1960s, Kinzua State Park has been a destination for tourists to see the incredible feat of engineering known as the Kinzua Viaduct, once the tallest railroad bridge in the world. However, one fateful day in 2003, the historic viaduct was destroyed in a powerful tornado. Rather than rebuild the structure, the Pennsylvania Department of Natural Resources converted the remains into a skywalk and visitor center where visitors can learn about the history of the logging industry in the region. The remains of the once-soaring bridge now live as a viewing platform where you can look out over the rolling hills of the rugged valley.

You'll begin your trek at the visitor center; be sure to carve out some time to explore the two floors of exhibitions highlighting the area's history of industry and its ecological impacts. From the visitor center, you'll start on the concrete ramp that snakes down alongside the building. At the bottom of the hill, to the left is the famous Skywalk, which you'll come back to at the end of the hike. You'll continue down

the Kinzua Creek Trail, passing observation platforms complete with binoculars and an interpretative sign about the viaduct. The terms bridge and viaduct are used interchangeably throughout the park, but a viaduct refers to a type of long narrow bridge that typically spans a valley through a series of arches. The Kinzua Viaduct once stood 2,053 feet long and 301 feet high. From the first observation platform, you'll follow a series of switchbacks down the steep hillside. There are large rocks embedded in the trail that make for some hefty steps.

After around a half mile, the trail lets out onto a stream and small bridge leading to the fallen bridge structure. You'll pass by a solid concrete pier, which is over 6 feet high. The trail officially ends here and for your safety, the park prohibits visitors from getting closer to the bridge debris. Although you'll see foraged paths, please be mindful not to venture off the trail and obey any danger signs. As you look at the twisted metal remains, rest easy knowing that the bridge had been closed to industrial traffic for years before the tornado.

After exploring, you'll return up the steep trail. Make sure to have plenty of water and take rests, as this trail offers little shade and can be very intense. About a mile in, the trail swings close to one of the remaining bridge trusses, which supports the Skywalk. Looking up, the sheer size of these steel monoliths is staggering. The viaduct was originally built in 1881 to expedite shipping from McKean County's rich oil, timber, and coal mines to manufacturers in the Great Lakes region. Although originally made of iron, it was rebuilt only 20 years later with steel to support the weight of heavier trains.

After returning all the way to the top of the hill, you'll end your outing at the Skywalk. This towering observation platform is built on the reinforced remains of the viaduct. Be prepared for a sudden change in temperature as wind whips around the exposed platform. At the very end, you can peer down at the trusses through a section of clear flooring. The view from the deck offers an unparalleled panorama of the surrounding Appalachian Plateau and is a top destination for fall foliage. After getting your fill of the stunning landscape, finish out your hike by walking back along the Skywalk to the parking lot.

## TURN-BY-TURN DIRECTIONS

1. From the wooden trail kiosk outside the visitor center, start down the paved path following the signposts for Skywalk and Observation platforms.
2. At 0.1 miles, turn right to take the gravel trail along the wooden fence, following the signs for observation platforms and Kinzua Creek Trail.
3. At 0.2 miles, reach the first observation platform. Explore the multiple levels, then return to the trail. Turn right down the marked Kinzua Creek Trail.
4. At 0.5 miles, use the bridge to cross the small creek.
5. At 0.6 miles, reach the end of the Kinzua Creek Trail. After observing the fallen bridge, retrace your steps back up the trail.
6. At 0.9 miles, turn right to follow a side branch of the Kinzua Creek Trail to an observation platform underneath the bridge. Afterward, continue uphill on the trail until it rejoins the main section of the Kinzua Creek Trail in 200 feet.
7. At 1.1 miles, reach the same intersection from Step 2. This time, keep right, following the signs for the Skywalk. In 100 feet, turn right onto the wooden platform with railroad tracks down the center.
8. At 1.2 miles, reach the furthest point on the platform. After taking in the surrounding scenery, return back along the rail tracks and then follow the paved path back to the parking lot to complete the hike.

## FIND THE TRAILHEAD

From Kane, take US-6 East. In 12.2 miles, turn left onto Lower Lindholm Road. There is no signage for this road and it comes up quickly. Continue on Lower Lindholm Road for 0.7 miles; then turn right at the stop sign onto Lindholm Road. In 2.3 miles, turn left onto Viaduct Road at the large "Kinzua Bridge State Park" sign. Pass over the train tracks, then proceed for 0.7 miles. The road ends at the large parking lot for the visitor center. The hike begins at the informational kiosk directly to the left of the visitor center.

# LOGYARD BREWING

Walking into Logyard Brewing feels like walking into a time capsule thanks to the antique tools and historic photos of the local logging industry adorning the walls. For owners Michael Dunn, Royce Novosel-Johnson, and Timothy Robinson, the brewery pays homage to the deeply engrained logging industry in Kane. In fact, the brewery sits next to a building that housed Novosel-Johnson's family logging business for over 60 years. Logyard officially opened in 2019 and from a humble seed, it has grown to distribute across the whole state.

The lumber industry isn't just evident in the décor; it's in the beer, too! Logyard uses a tincture from birch trees to make their Bucking Birch Ale. It's worth going out on a limb to try this peculiar flavor profile. For a more classic style, the Greenhorn Session IPA is an easy-drinking IPA that doesn't skimp on flavor. Named for a rookie on the jobsite, this brew is sure to be a hit with both novice and expert craft beer lovers.

With the range of taps available, it can be hard to choose just one. Thankfully you don't have to! You can order a 12-pour flight of every item on the taplist, served in a hewn birch log. When visiting Kane, a stop at Logyard Brewing is a clear-cut choice.

## LAND MANAGER

**PA Department of Conservation & Natural Resources**
296 Viaduct Road
Kane, PA 16735
(814) 778-5467
www.dcnr.pa.gov/StateParks/FindAPark/KinzuaBridgeStatePark
Map: elibrary.dcnr.pa.gov/GetDocument?docId=1737574&DocName=KINZ_ParkMap.pdf

## BREWERY/RESTAURANT

**Logyard Brewing**
103 North Fraley Street
Kane, PA 16735
(814) 757-6070
www.logyardbrewing.com

Distance from trailhead: 16 miles

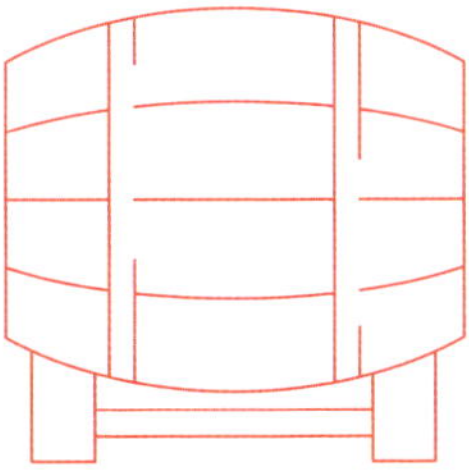

# MOUNT NITTANY

## CLIMB TO SOARING VIEWS OF HAPPY VALLEY

| STARTING POINT | DESTINATION |
|---|---|
| MOUNT NITTANY TRAILHEAD PARKING | MOUNT NITTANY |

| BREWERY | HIKE TYPE |
|---|---|
| HAPPY VALLEY BREWING COMPANY | MODERATE |

| DOG-FRIENDLY | SEASON |
|---|---|
| YES (LEASH REQUIRED) | YEAR-ROUND |

| FEES | DURATION |
|---|---|
| NONE | 2 HOURS 30 MIN. |

| MAP REFERENCE | LENGTH |
|---|---|
| POSTED AT TRAILHEAD | 4.7 MILES (LOOP) |

| HIGHLIGHTS | ELEVATION GAIN |
|---|---|
| VIEWS OF PENN STATE, WILDLIFE | 940 FEET |

**4.7 %**
ALCOHOL CONTENT

## TAILGATER PALE ALE

CLOUDY ORANGE

CITRUS

HOPPY

BITTERNESS SWEETNESS

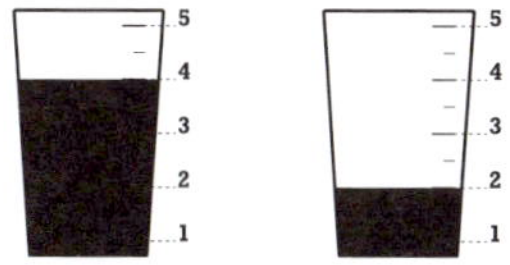


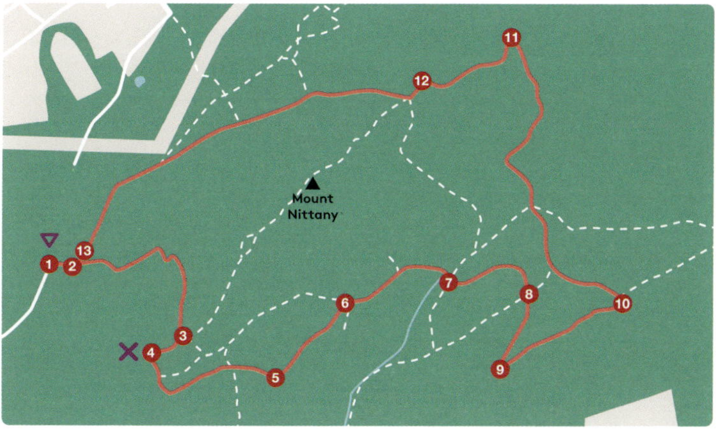


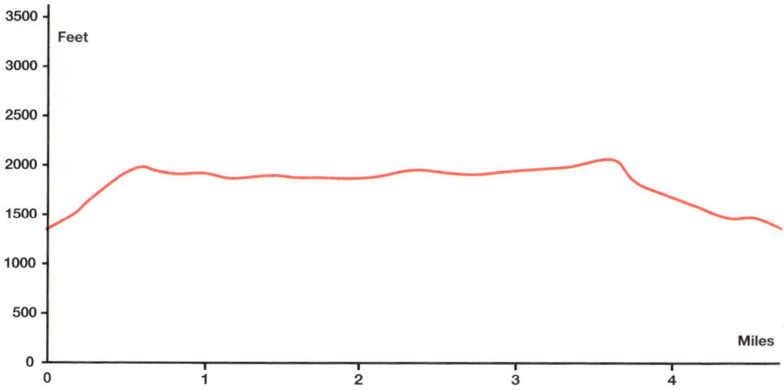

# HIKE DESCRIPTION

**Climb Centre County's most popular trail for lofty views of Happy Valley, home to Penn State University. After enjoying the hard-earned vistas, head to Happy Valley Brewing Company for a hearty meal and brew in a converted barn with a beer-inspired ceiling mural.**

A visit to State College can't be complete without a visit to Mount Nittany. The mountain is the namesake for the celebrated "Nittany Lion" mascot of the largest university in Pennsylvania. While there are several legends and folklore about where the name "Nittany" comes from, it is generally thought to come from the Algonquian people's native name for the ridge, which is *Nekti-Attin*, meaning single mountain. While it's geologically too small to be a true mountain, Mount Nittany is still an excellent place for views of PSU and the affectionately named Happy Valley.

This area is maintained by the Mount Nittany Conservancy, a non-profit originally formed by Penn State alumni to save the ridge from the logging industry in the 1940s. Again in the 1980s, the land was under threat by developers, so the Conservancy purchased and preserved more of the mountain. Today, the Mountain Nittany Conservancy cares for over 300 acres of land and works with other landowners toward the long-term preservation of the mountain.

While there are over 8 miles of intersecting trails on Mount Nittany, this 5 mile loop circles the peak, stopping by each of the best overlooks. When planning this hike, it's important to remember that it's popular both with locals and Penn State's large student population. It's a good idea to visit at off peak times. The trailhead is in a residential area, so be mindful of where you park and don't block access to homes.

You'll start the hike on the Blue/White Trail which leads straight up a very rocky hillside. You'll want plenty of water for the trek and be aware of the temperature and humidity for the day, as this trail gains over 600 feet of rocky elevation in half a mile! Throughout the hike you'll find helpful maps showing the exact map reference for your current location. There are also several "shortcut" trails if the full loop feels like too much.

After making it up the initial incline, you'll reach the Mike Lynch overlook, which boasts views of the PSU campus. After this first overlook, you'll travel along the wooded and rocky Blue-Blazed Trail that skirts around the hill for the rest of the hike. You'll pass other overlooks offering numerous views of the surrounding valley. The trail is relatively easy for the remainder of the hike and is a great place for viewing wildflowers and mushrooms. During spring showers, keep an eye out for tiny red eastern newts whose bright orange/red color warns of their toxicity and who only spend a quarter of their life on land. Nearing the end of the circle around the summit, you'll reach the Nittany Mall overlook. This is the last of the overlooks and arguably the nicest. You'll find a huge rock perfect for sitting, with trees that frame the vista. From the overlook, take your time navigating the rocky descent as you return the way you came.

## TURN-BY-TURN DIRECTIONS

1. From the kiosk at the trailhead, continue up the path marked by white blazes.
2. At 0.1 miles, turn right on the White Trail marked by white blazes on trees to start the loop.
3. At 0.5 miles, turn right onto the Blue Trail, now following the blue blazes.
4. At 0.7 miles, reach the Mike Lynch Overlook. Find the Blue Trail again at the front left point of the overlook. Just after the overlook, bear right to stay on the Blue Trail.
5. At 1.1 miles, reach the Boalsburg Overlook. Continue on the Blue Trail.
6. At 1.3 miles, bear right to stay on the Blue Trail.
7. At 1.6 miles, reach a junction with the White Trail and continue straight to stay on the Blue Trail.
8. At 1.9 miles, cross over the mountain bike trail to stay on the Blue Trail.
9. At 2.1 miles, reach the Little Flat Overlook. Continue on the Blue Trail.
10. At 2.4 miles, reach Penn's Valley Viewpoint. Continue on the Blue Trail.
11. At 3.3 miles, reach the Spring Creek Watergap Overlook. Continue on the Blue Trail.
12. At 3.6 miles, reach the Nittany Mall Overlook. Just past the overlook, turn right onto the Blue Trail.
13. At 4.6 miles, turn right onto the White Trail to return to the parking lot.

# FIND THE TRAILHEAD

From State College, go northeast on East College Street/PA-26 N. Continue for 1.3 miles, then turn slightly right onto Elmwood Street. After 0.7 miles, turn left onto Pike Street. In 0.1 miles, turn right onto Mount Nittany Road; proceed for 0.7 miles. There will be a slight left to stay on Mount Nittany Road that leads directly to the trailhead. If the parking is full, follow the signs for overflow parking at the opposite end of the street.

# HAPPY VALLEY BREWING COMPANY

Happy Valley Brewing Company is in an old barn and all of the details and decor nod to the building's previous life as a dairy farm, with exposed wood beams and animal sculptures crafted from chicken wire. Even the old wooden sign for Klinger's Farm sits proudly above the bar! While you're looking, take a gaze at the ceiling mural and you'll get a chuckle out of the beer-minded constellations.

The brewery and restaurant feature two floors with a more traditional restaurant when you first walk in and a downstairs lounge with live music and a relaxed vibe. Both levels have the full kitchen menu specializing in pub favorites along with a more sophisticated farm-to-table menu that rotates seasonally and features ingredients from local farms and small businesses. Named as a nod to football weekends, the Tailgater Pale Ale is a delightfully hoppy ale with a slight tangerine flavor. Coming in at a low 4.7% ABV, this beer is made for a perfect post-hike lunchtime pour.

## LAND MANAGER

**Mount Nittany Conservancy**
P.O. Box 334
State College, PA 16804
(814) 237-0400
www.nittany.org
Map: nittany.org/wp-content/uploads/2023/05/2023-MNC-Brochure.pdf

## BREWERY/RESTAURANT

**Happy Valley Brewing Company**
137 Elmwood Street
State College, PA 16801
(814) 234-4406
www.happyvalleybeer.com

Distance from trailhead: 1.4 miles

# HAWK ROCK

## HIKE TO STUNNING VIEWS OF THE SUSQUEHANNA RIVER

DUNCANNON, PA

| STARTING POINT | DESTINATION |
| --- | --- |
| HAWK ROCK PARKING AREA | HAWK ROCK OVERLOOK |
| **BREWERY** | **HIKE TYPE** |
| PIZZA BOY BREWING | STRENUOUS |
| **DOG-FRIENDLY** | **SEASON** |
| YES (LEASH REQUIRED) | YEAR-ROUND |
| **FEES** | **DURATION** |
| NO | 1 HOUR |
| **MAP REFERENCE** | **LENGTH** |
| POSTED AT TRAILHEAD | 1.6 MILES (ROUND TRIP) |
| **HIGHLIGHTS** | **ELEVATION GAIN** |
| APPALACHIAN TRAIL, OVERLOOK | 760 FEET |

**4.4 %** ALCOHOL CONTENT

**LEMON SHANDY**

**BRIGHT YELLOW**

**SWEET, CITRUS**

**CRISP**

**BITTERNESS** **SWEETNESS**

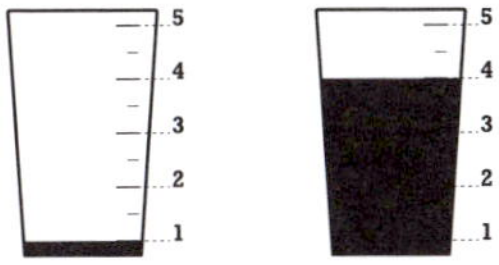


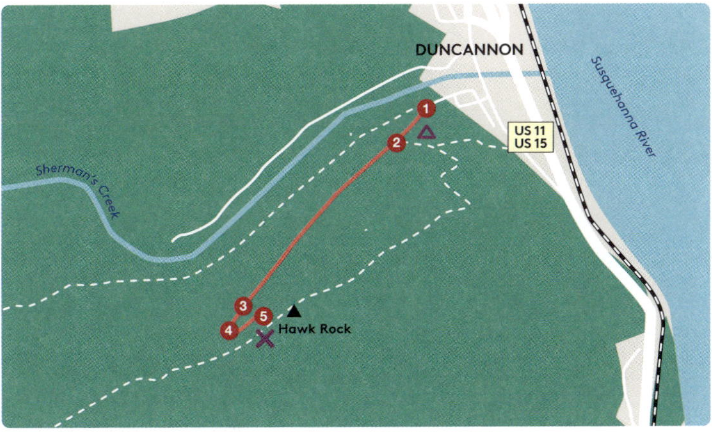


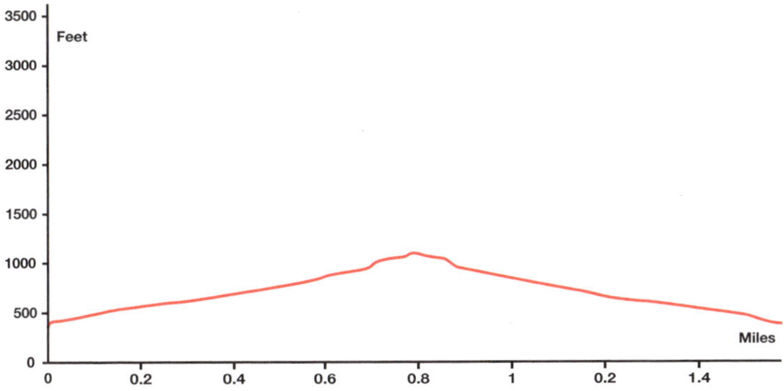

# HIKE DESCRIPTION

**Take this short hike near the midpoint of the Appalachian Trail for a taste of "Rocksylvania" and for stunning views of the Susquehanna River. Afterwards, head over to Pizza Boy Brewing for an enormous variety of tasty beers.**

As part of its nearly 2,200-mile journey, the Appalachian Trail (AT) meanders 229 miles through Pennsylvania. However, you don't need to hike all of that for beautiful views of the state—this short but steep segment just north of Harrisburg will give you a breathtaking taste as you reach the scenic viewpoint called Hawk Rock.

At the trailhead, you'll find some interpretive signs about the rugged geology of the region and the wildlife you may encounter, like painted turtles and garter snakes. You'll begin the hike ascending a steep dirt trail for around 500 feet until you meet up with the Appalachian Trail on the left. While the hike to the overlook is less than a mile, it gains

over 700 feet of elevation along rocky, uneven terrain. Take your time, bring plenty of water, and enjoy a little taste of what AT thru-hikers wryly refer to as "Rocksylvania." Starting near Duncannon, the AT shifts from compact dirt trails to endless rock paths heading up and down the inclines of the Kittatinny Ridge—Pennsylvania's section of the Appalachian Mountains.

As you ascend to the Hawk Rock overlook, the terrain shifts from large stone steps to paths of rocks ranging in size from a fist to football. The rock-strewn way makes for a potentially ankle-twisting trek, so poles and proper footwear are essential. At the very top, the trail bends to the left and opens onto the huge sandstone rock outcropping of Hawk Rock. Below lies Sherman Creek and the town of Duncannon, which is a popular rest spot for AT thru-hikers. To the right is where the Juniata River flows into the massive Susquehanna River along its journey from New York to the Chesapeake Bay. After enjoying the sweeping views, turn around and navigate back down the hill to the parking lot.

## TURN-BY-TURN DIRECTIONS

1. From the kiosk at the trailhead parking lot, continue straight ahead on the trail directly to the left of the large signpost for Hawk Rock overlook.
2. At 0.1 miles, reach the T-junction with the white-marked Appalachian Trail coming from the left. Get on the AT and continue straight up the trail.
3. At 0.6 miles, cross through a rock field and continue straight.
4. At 0.7 miles, climb the rock stairs for the steepest part of the trail.
5. At. 0.8 miles, the trail opens up onto a rocky expanse. To the left is the overlook. Return the way you came back to the parking lot.

# FIND THE TRAILHEAD

From Harrisburg, get on I-81 S. After crossing the Wade Memorial Bridge, take Exit 65 to merge onto US-11 N/US-15 N toward Marysville. Stay on US-11/US-15 for 9.2 miles, then take the exit for Duncannon/274 West. At the end of the off-ramp, keep left at the fork, following signs for the Recycling Center. After 100 feet, turn left onto S. Main Street. After 0.3 miles, turn right onto Little Boston Road and then immediately turn right onto Watershed Drive. The large parking lot will be at the end of the road in 0.1 miles, marked by a sign for the Duncannon Watershed where the trail begins.

# PIZZA BOY BREWING

While Pizza Boy Brewing is a well-known name in the Pennsylvania beer scene, the pizza came first. Owner Albert Kominski opened his self-described "hole-in-the-wall" pizza restaurant, Als of Hampden, in 2002 offering craft beer on draft and in bottles alongside his pizzas. After years of curating a wide selection of brews, Kominski decided to start an in-house line of beer in 2011. The brewery quickly became popular and outgrew their old pizza shop.

In 2012, the team upgraded to their current space, a large warehouse facility in Enola, Pennsylvania where they have a full menu for eat-in and take-out and over 100 beers on tap! The brewery always offers a huge variety of Pizza Boy beers along with other local favorites and standard domestic pours. In addition to a hefty lineup of year-round staples, Pizza Boy often has limited releases featuring unique ingredients like chili peppers or locally-foraged pawpaws. For summer in a glass, try the Lemon Shandy, which is the perfect thirst-quencher after the steep hike to Hawk Rock.

## LAND MANAGER

**Appalachian Trail Conservancy**
799 Washington Street, PO Box 807
Harpers Ferry, WV 25425
(304) 535-6331
www.appalachiantrail.org
Map: www.visithersheyharrisburg.org/trails/adventure-trail/hiking/hawk-rock/

## BREWERY/RESTAURANT

**Al's of Hampden/Pizza Boy Brewing Company**
2240 Millennium Way
Enola, PA 17025
(717) 728-3840
www.alsofhampden.com

Distance from trailhead: 13.7 miles

# WILDWOOD PARK

## A WILDLIFE SANCTUARY IN PENNSYLVANIA'S CAPITAL CITY

| STARTING POINT | DESTINATION |
|---|---|
| WILDWOOD PARK NORTH LOT | WILDWOOD LAKE |
| **BREWERY** | **HIKE TYPE** |
| ZERODAY BREWING COMPANY | EASY |
| **DOG-FRIENDLY** | **SEASON** |
| YES (LEASH REQUIRED) | YEAR-ROUND |
| **FEES** | **DURATION** |
| NONE | 1 HOUR 15 MIN. |
| **MAP REFERENCE** | **LENGTH** |
| POSTED AT TRAILHEAD | 3.2 MILES (LOOP) |
| **HIGHLIGHTS** | **ELEVATION GAIN** |
| BIRDWATCHING, SPILLWAYS | 154 FEET |

4.1% ALCOHOL CONTENT

**BLUE COLLAR HIPSTER SESSION IPA**

CLEAR GOLD

LIGHT

FLORAL

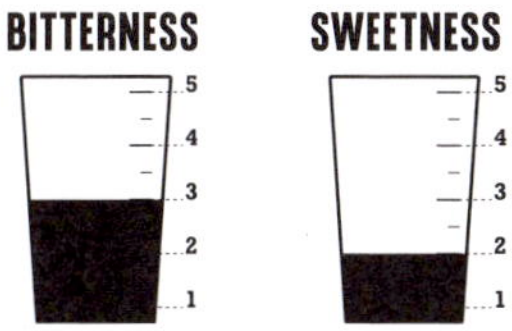


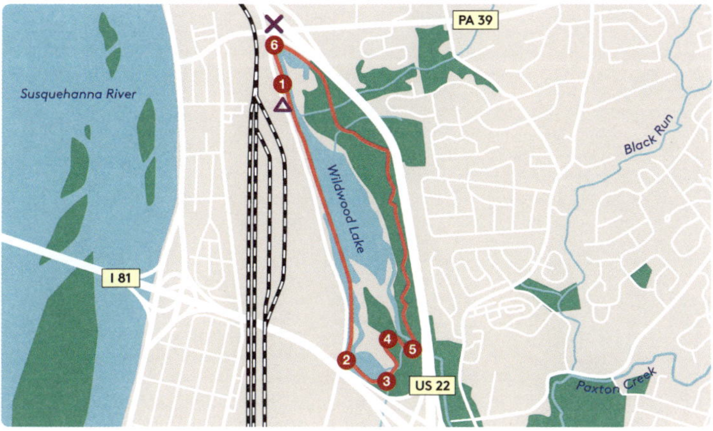


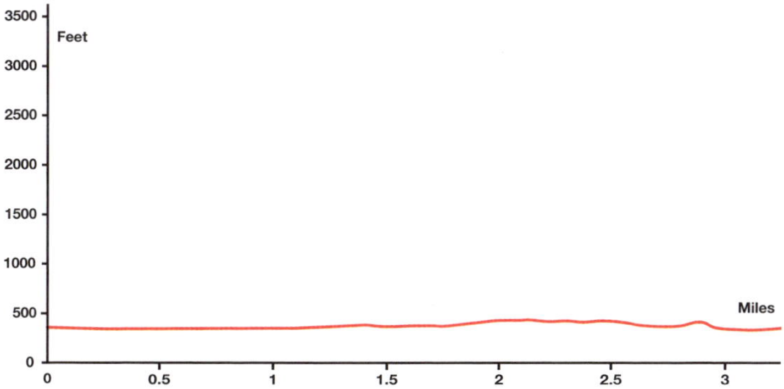

# HIKE DESCRIPTION

**Spot birds and other wildlife in the heart of Pennsylvania's state capital while meandering through this peaceful nature preserve. Afterward, relax with a pour of Blue-Collar Hipster from thru-hikers turned full-time brewers at Zeroday Brewing.**

Maintained by Dauphin County Parks and Recreation, Wildwood Park is a peaceful oasis in the heart of a busy political center. With miles of boardwalks and paved trails, Wildwood Park offers a perfect outing for hikers of all levels. While the park is popular with birders and nature-lovers, it also functions as flood prevention for the city, so you'll see unique features like spillways on the lake. Spillways are man-made features that prevent flooding by diverting overflow rainwater underground to a nearby body of water—in this case, the Susquehanna River.

Although the City of Harrisburg established the original park in the early 1900s, decades of neglect turned it into a swampy mess. Finally, the county government purchased the land in the 1980s, and Wildwood saw a decade of revitalization. Now, it's a beautiful wetland park that feels like a secluded "wild" haven bursting with biodiversity, despite the surrounding highways.

Setting out on this easy loop along a flat trail, you'll see the lake on your left and the remnants of the Pennsylvania Canal on your right. The shallow and rocky waters of the Susquehanna River were nearly impossible to transport goods so, in the 1800s, the canal was built as a key transportation method across the state. Plodding along beside the canal, mules towed cargo in boats along a towpath. While you meander on the remains of this towpath, keep an eye on either side and you might see some aquatic friends like painted turtles, great egrets, and bullfrogs in the water. At the end of the towpath, the trail becomes the paved Wildwood Way following around the lake and past the Morning Glory Spillway. Stop by the interpretive sign in front of the water to learn about how spillways protect delicate ecosystems from erosion. From here, you can choose from a variety of trails, but for this loop, you'll walk the Delta Boardwalk, which brings you right into the wetland environment. These marshy ecosystems help to filter debris and pollution from water while also acting like a sponge to prevent flooding. The tall grasses and cattails also provide a habitat for nesting waterfowl like mallards and red-winged blackbirds. From the boardwalk, you'll continue on the Wildwood Way Trail to complete the loop around the lake. Just before reaching the parking lot, look for the impressive Susquehanna Spillway on your left side, creating a rectangle of cascading water.

## TURN-BY-TURN DIRECTIONS

1. From the North Parking Lot, follow the signposted Towpath Trail heading to the right.
2. At 1.1 miles, pass a restroom building and then turn left onto the Wildwood Trail.
3. At 1.3 miles, pass the Morning Glory Spillway. Just after this feature, turn left onto the signposted Delta Boardwalk.
4. At 1.5 miles, turn right to stay on the boardwalk.
5. At 1.6 miles at the end of the boardwalk, turn left to get back on the paved Wildwood Trail which continues along the lake.
6. At 3.1 miles, reach the Susquehanna Spillway on the left. Continue on the Wildwood Trail until it meets up with the North Parking Lot.

## FIND THE TRAILHEAD

From I-81 in Harrisburg, take Exit 66 for N. Front Street. At the end of the off-ramp, keep left and merge onto N. Front Street. After 0.7 miles, turn right onto Linglestown Road (PA-39E). In 0.4 miles, make a right onto Industrial Drive. After 0.2 miles, the North Parking Lot will be on the left with a large green sign.

# ZERODAY BREWING COMPANY

Zeroday Brewing has been a staple of the Harrisburg beer scene since 2017 and now it has three separate outposts and taprooms throughout the state capitol. The main taproom on North 3rd street boasts a beer garden, event space, spacious taproom, and full kitchen menu.

Zeroday Brewing is a particularly great place to pair with a hike because the founders Theo and Brandalynn Armstrong are avid hikers. The brewery name was actually inspired by Theo's Appalachian Trail thru-hike—a "zero day" is a backpacking term for a day of no miles traveled, just relaxing and recharging. For the team at this brewery, the name's a reminder to take a break and explore some of the "side trails life has to offer." Cheers to that!

Blue Collar Hipster is a session IPA that's low on the ABV but not on flavor. With notes of white grape and nectarine, there's a bright peppery flavor that keeps you on your toes. This light brew is a perfect thirst quencher after a day out on the trails.

## LAND MANAGER

**Dauphin County Parks and Recreation**
100 Fort Hunter Road,
Harrisburg, PA 17110
(717) 599-5188
www.dauphincounty.gov
Map: explorewildwoodpark.org/about/wildwood-park-nature-trails

## BREWERY/RESTAURANT

**Zeroday Brewing Company**
925 North 3rd Street
Harrisburg, PA 17102
(717) 745-6218
www.zerodaybrewing.com

Distance from trailhead: 5.2 miles

# PINE CREEK GORGE

## CLAMBER INTO PENNSYLVANIA'S OWN "GRAND CANYON"

| STARTING POINT | DESTINATION |
|---|---|
| LEONARD HARRISON STATE PARK VISITOR CENTER | PINE CREEK GORGE |
| **BREWERY** | **HIKE TYPE** |
| WELLSBORO HOUSE RESTAURANT & BREWERY | MODERATE |
| **DOG-FRIENDLY** | **SEASON** |
| YES (LEASH REQUIRED) | APRIL–NOVEMBER |
| **FEES** | **DURATION** |
| NONE | 2 HOURS |
| **MAP REFERENCE** | **LENGTH** |
| POSTED AT VISITOR CENTER | 3 MILES (ROUND TRIP) |
| **HIGHLIGHTS** | **ELEVATION GAIN** |
| WATERFALL, SCENIC VISTAS, CREEK | 958 FEET |

5.5 %
ALCOHOL CONTENT

## DAN SMITH'S CHOCOLATE STOUT

DARK BROWN

CHOCOLATE

CHOCOLATE MILK

BITTERNESS

SWEETNESS

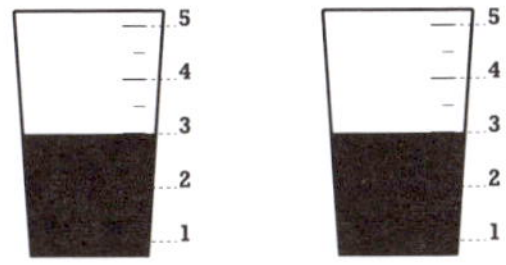


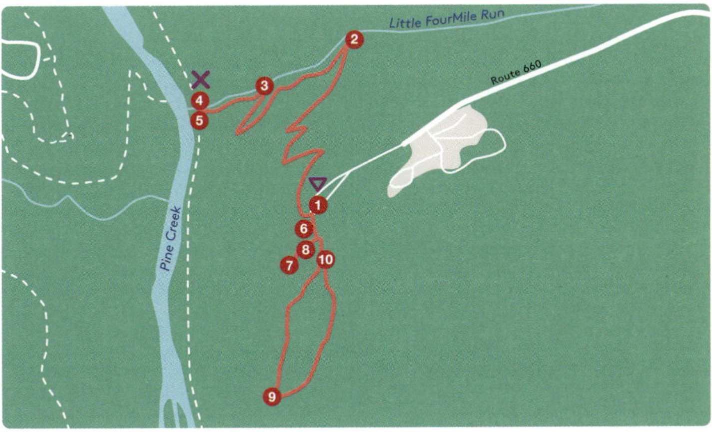


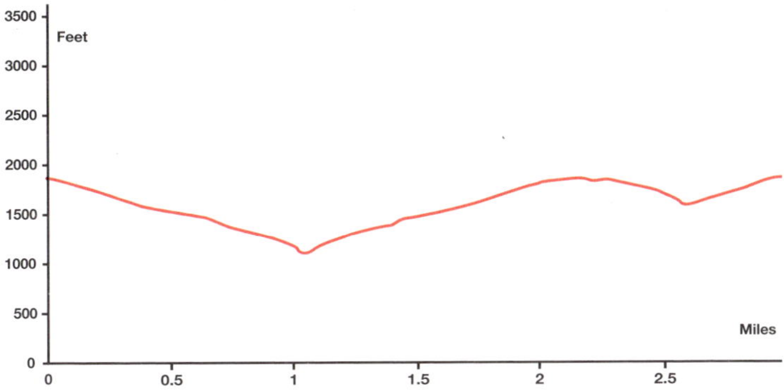

# HIKE DESCRIPTION

**Navigate the Pine Creek Gorge—also known as the Pennsylvania Grand Canyon—for breathtaking views of waterfalls and tree-lined cliffs. After, unwind in downtown Wellsboro at Wellsboro House with some local brews in a restored 1862 building.**

The Pennsylvania Grand Canyon, plunging over 1,400 feet at its deepest point, was carved out by a 47-mile section of Pine Creek. Leonard Harrison State Park preserves over 500 acres as a National Natural Landmark with Colton State Park to the west.

The park underwent renovations in 2023 and now sports a new visitor center with exhibits about local history and ecology, as well as an expanded accessible parking lot. This hike starts at the visitor center and follows the large signs for the Turkey Path. You'll notice signs about danger due to a cliff side, so proceed down the trail with caution. Immediately, the trail descends wooden steps and natural paths deep into the gorge. Along the way, you'll find scenic stops to view waterfalls along Little Four-Mile Run, a small tributary of Pine Creek. At the bottom of the final set of stairs, the Turkey Path lets out onto the Pine Creek Rail Trail. This long-distance bike trail follows what was once an important trade route for Native Americans and then a key rail line for the logging industry. You'll cross the bike path to follow a small, unmarked trail down to the water for incredible views of the canyon. While looking at the tree-lined gorge, it's hard to imagine that 100 years ago, the logging industry caused mass deforestation and habitat loss. Thankfully, revitalization efforts paid off and now the forest is once again home to elk, otters, bald eagles, and beavers.

After taking in the canyon, be prepared for a heart-pumping hike back up the hillside, climbing 800 feet in 1 mile. Once at the top, you'll have an easy 1-mile loop on a wide dirt path to view the stunning overlooks that peer deep down into the gorge.

## TURN-BY-TURN DIRECTIONS

1. Begin at the Leonard Harrison State Park Visitor Center. Immediately turn right onto the Turkey Path, marked with a large wooden sign.
2. At 0.5 miles, encounter a waterfall viewpoint and then continue down the Turkey Path.
3. At 0.9 miles, reach another view of a waterfall along Little Four-mile Run and then continue down the Turkey Path.
4. At 1.0 miles, after a flight of stairs, the trail opens onto the Rail Trail. See the waterfall to the right, then cross the Rail Trail to access the creek on a small, unmarked trail.
5. At 1.1 miles, where the trail meets the creek, turn around and return up the Turkey Path back to the visitor center.
6. At 2.1 miles, continue straight past the visitor center at the top of the Turkey Path to access the Overlook Trail of the canyon. Continue straight along the fence.

7. At 2.2 miles, at a flight of stairs, take the steps down to a large viewing platform. Once you've had your fill of the view, return to the top of the stairs, and turn right back onto the unmarked Overlook Trail.
8. At 2.6 miles, reach the Otter View platform and continue along the Overlook Trail.
9. At 2.9 miles, turn right to complete the Overlook Trail loop. Continue straight back to the visitor center.

## FIND THE TRAILHEAD

From Wellsboro, take Route 660W for 5 miles, then turn left to stay on Route 660W. After 0.4 miles, turn left to continue on 660W. In 2 mile, reach a junction and turn left to stay on 660W. After 1 mile, bear left at the intersection to continue on 660W. After 2 miles, the route passes into the state park. Follow the signs for overlooks to pass through the roundabout next to the park office. Directly ahead is the parking lot. The trail begins at the visitor center at the southwest corner of the parking lot.

# WELLSBORO HOUSE RESTAURANT & BREWERY

Chris and Laura Kozuhowski opened their popular restaurant in 2008 after lovingly restoring the 1862 former hotel. The couple prioritized retaining original features, which they found especially important because the town is a historic district on the National Register of Historic Places. As you enjoy a pint at the original wooden bar, notice the notches and scratches of nearly 160 years of thirsty travelers that visited the hotel.

After growing into a popular neighborhood spot, the Kozuhowskis began adding house-made beer to their menu and officially became the Wellsboro House Restaurant & Brewery in 2013. Starting out with only two taps, they quickly grew and now brew in a 1914 train depot just across the street from the main restaurant, giving new life to the town's connection to the Pennsylvania rail lines. A visit to Wellsboro House wouldn't be complete without a taste of Dan Smith's Chocolate Stout, made with real chocolates from the popular Dan Smith's Chocolates in Brookeville, PA. This delightful treat offers a sweet taste without too much heaviness.

## LAND MANAGER

**PA Department of Natural Resources**
4797 Route 660
Wellsboro, PA 16901-8970
(570) 724-3061
www.dcnr.pa.gov/StateParks/FindAPark/LeonardHarrisonStatePark
Map: elibrary.dcnr.pa.gov/GetDocument?docId=1753215&DocName=LEHA_COLT_ParkMap.pdf

## BREWERY/RESTAURANT

**Wellsboro House Restaurant & Brewery**
34 Charleston Street
Wellsboro, PA 16901
www.thewellsborohouse.com
(570) 723-4687

Distance from trailhead: 11 miles

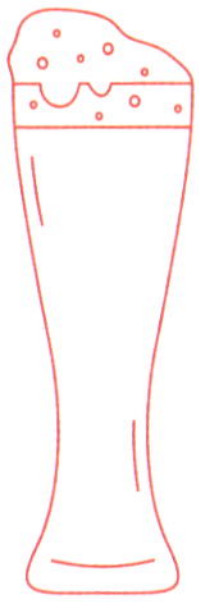

# SMITH KNOB

## HIKE TO A BREATHTAKING SECLUDED OVERLOOK

**STARTING POINT**

PAINTER RUN TRAIL PARKING

**BREWERY**

NEW TRAIL BREWING CO.

**DOG-FRIENDLY**

YES (LEASH REQUIRED)

**FEES**

NONE

**MAP REFERENCE**

POSTED AT TRAILHEAD

**HIGHLIGHTS**

LOYALSOCK CREEK, LOYALSOCK TRAIL (LT)

**DESTINATION**

SMITH KNOB

**HIKE TYPE**

STRENUOUS

**SEASON**

YEAR-ROUND

**DURATION**

2 HOURS 30 MIN.

**LENGTH**

4.5 MILES (LOOP)

**ELEVATION GAIN**

1,300 FEET

7.0 %
ALCOHOL CONTENT

## ROCKSYLVANIA IPA

CLEAR GOLD

TROPICAL

JUICY CITRUS

BITTERNESS

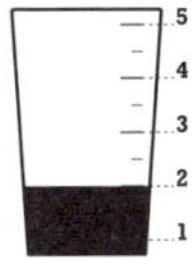


SWEETNESS

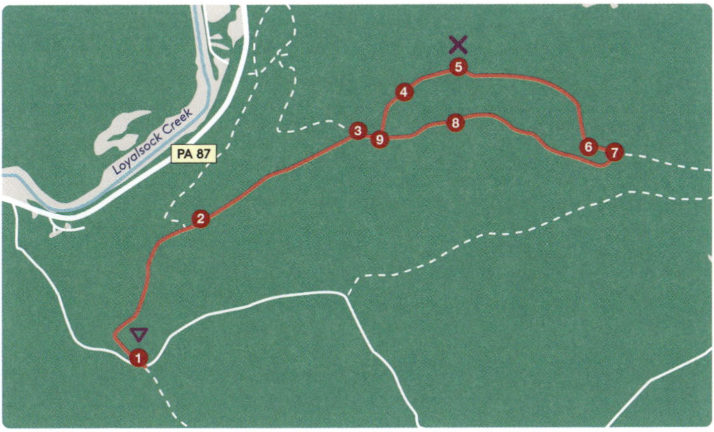


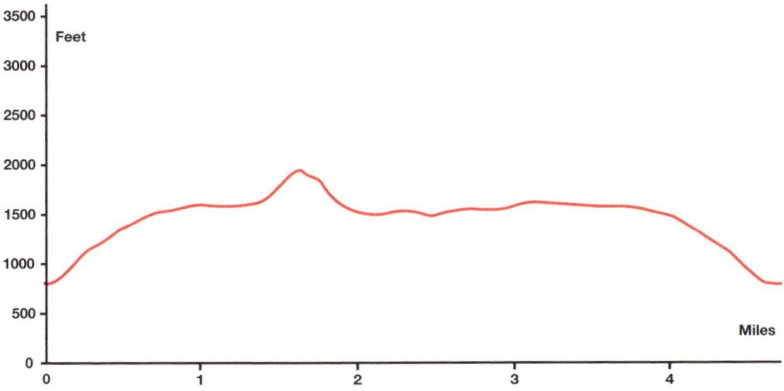

# HIKE DESCRIPTION

**Enjoy a stunning overlook on a portion of the 59-mile Loyalsock Trail through Loyalsock State Forest. After your challenging adventure, reward yourself with a post-hike brew at New Trail Brewing Co.**

Loyalsock State Forest is one of 20 state forests in Pennsylvania. It spans over 114,000 acres across Bradford, Sullivan, and Lycoming counties. Part of the Endless Mountain region, the forest is named for the scenic Loyalsock creek that runs through the center. There's more than 200 miles of hiking in the Loyalsock State Forest but the most popular is the Loyalsock backpacking trail. Thankfully, there are several parking access points so it's also accessible for day hikes!

The Loyalsock Trail (LT) dates back to the 1950s and is maintained today by the Alpine Club of Williamsport. With over 11,000 feet of elevation gain, the 59-mile trail is a true challenge. The day hike to Smith's Knob starts near the Western terminus of the LT off the unpaved Little Bear Creek Road. Access along this road may be difficult in the winter months. The parking lot is very large but there are no bathroom facilities, so plan accordingly.

Throughout this hike, small metal discs on trees denote the trail, so look for the red LT emblazoned on a yellow background. From the parking lot, the dirt trail climbs nearly 700 feet in a half-mile. However, the many viewpoints along the trail make the challenging climb well worth it! Around a half-mile in, you'll reach the first vista, Helen's Window. While not the most impressive view, it's a nice spot to catch your breath.

A little under a mile after Helen's Window, after crossing a trail intersection, you'll get to the final push to the Knob. Here, the trail becomes especially steep and rocky, and you may need all four limbs to get up there. At the top, just past the backpacking campsite and to the left is the Smith's Knob Overlook. Gazing out over the rolling hills and creek deep in the valley feels incredibly rewarding after the difficult trek.

From the overlook, you'll continue along the LT as it descends from the Knob. The next mile is a peaceful trek through hardwood forests with soaring birch, oak, and beech trees. Eventually, you'll meet up with a wide and flat bypass trail that will lead you back to the trailhead. The trail can get sunny and warm so take your time as you meander back to intersect with the LT and return to the parking lot.

## TURN-BY-TURN DIRECTIONS

1. From the parking lot, cross Little Bear Creek Road and head up the trail marked by a post with a red and yellow LT. Almost immediately, the trail opens onto a maintenance garage. Pass the garage and pick up the trail again to the left of the lot.
2. At 0.6 miles, reach a break in the trees called Helen's Window Overlook and then continue up the steep trail.
3. At 1.3 miles, turn right at a junction. Then, in less than 0.1 miles, turn left up the hill to stay on the Loyalsock Trail. This is the start of the loop and the steepest section of trail.
4. At 1.5 miles, pass a grassy overlook spot on the right.
5. At 1.7 miles, crest the top of the mountain. To the left is a campsite and the main vista overlooking the Loyalsock Creek. From here, the trail quickly leads downhill.
6. At 2.3 miles, bear left at a junction. Do not take the X-marked trail.
7. At 2.4 miles, turn right to get on the Smith Knob Bypass Trail marked with a yellow circle and a red X.
8. At 3.0 miles, continue on the trail as it veers away from the fence and becomes more narrow and wooded.
9. At 3.3 miles, meet back up with the Loyalsock Trail to complete the loop. Retrace your steps along the Loyalsock Trail until it returns to the parking lot.

# FIND THE TRAILHEAD

From I-180E in Williamsport, take Exit 21 for PA-87N/Loyalsock Ave. Turn left at the traffic light at the end of the exit ramp onto N. Loyalsock Ave. Proceed for 9.3 miles, then turn right onto Little Bear Creek Road. This is a narrow gravel road so drive cautiously. In 0.8 miles, the parking lot will be to the right across a small bridge with a large trail kiosk. The trail starts to the left of the road and is clearly marked with a signpost.

# NEW TRAIL BREWING CO.

From a brewery internship in college, New Trail Brewing owner and head brewer Mike LaRosa always knew the endgame was his own brewery. After years of serving in various head brewer roles, he also began a consulting business to help new breweries get on their feet. So, when local restaurateurs approached him about a new start-up, he was all in. Originally called Williamsport Brewing, LaRosa envisioned a brewery with ecotourism and outdoor sports at its core. New Trail is a mecca for both beer and hiking lovers. From the artwork to the beer names, everything about this brewery is an ode to the great outdoors. The cavernous taproom not only features a huge outdoor space, but even has a swag shop filled with outdoor gear. At the bar, expect a lineup of the brewery's standards including the ever popular Broken Heels, along with some more adventurous brews only available in the taproom. And if you find a standard you love, New Trail now distributes across the whole state of Pennsylvania!

One of the rotating drafts, Rocksylvania Hazy IPA is fitting after tackling the rocky incline of the Loyalsock Trail. Plus, you can drink easy knowing that New Trail frequently uses their platform and proceeds to promote and support conservation efforts that protect the public lands we love.

## LAND MANAGER

**Alpine Club of Williamsport**
P.O. Box 501
Williamsport, PA 17703
www.alpineclubofwilliamsport.com
Map: elibrary.dcnr.pa.gov/GetDocument?docId=1743705&DocName=sf-PUd20.pdf

## BREWERY/RESTAURANT

**New Trail Brewing Co.**
240 Arch Street Building 18
Williamsport, PA 17701
(570) 980-9295
www.newtrailbrewing.com

Distance from trailhead: 19.6 miles

# EASTERN PENNSYLVANIA

# SALT SPRINGS WATERFALLS

## OLD-GROWTH FORESTS AND WATERFALLS IN THE ENDLESS MOUNTAINS

| STARTING POINT | DESTINATION |
|---|---|
| WHEATON HOUSE PARK OFFICE | FALL BROOK WATERFALLS |
| **BREWERY** | **HIKE TYPE** |
| ENDLESS BREWING | EASY |
| **DOG-FRIENDLY** | **SEASON** |
| YES (LEASH REQUIRED) | YEAR-ROUND |
| **FEES** | **DURATION** |
| NONE | 1 HOUR 30 MIN. |
| **MAP REFERENCE** | **LENGTH** |
| POSTED AT PARK OFFICE | 2 MILES (LOOP) |
| **HIGHLIGHTS** | **ELEVATION GAIN** |
| WATERFALLS, OLD-GROWTH HEMLOCK TREES | 200 FEET |

**5.0 %**
**ALCOHOL CONTENT**

## GRASSHOPPER PALE ALE

**GOLDEN**

**HOPPY**

**BITTER**

**BITTERNESS**

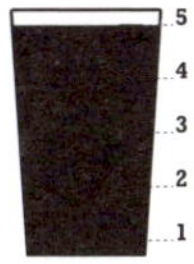


**SWEETNESS**

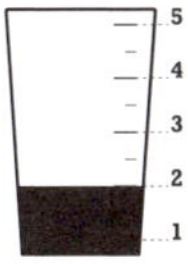


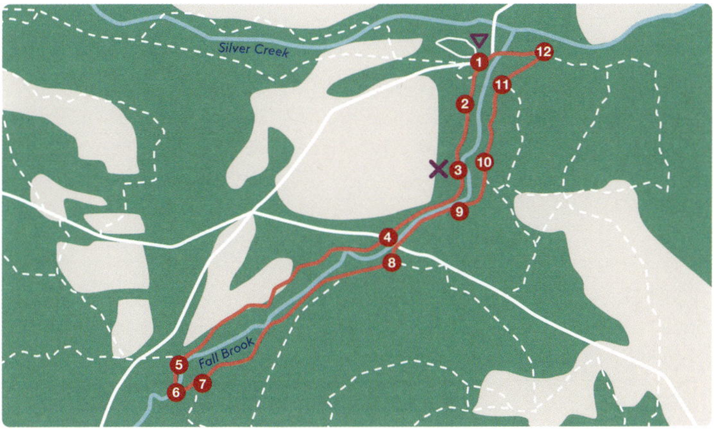


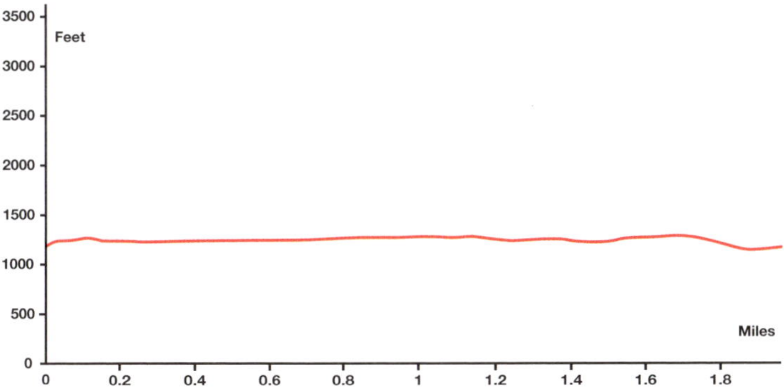

# HIKE DESCRIPTION

**Hike under towering hemlocks to three waterfalls on this easy hike in Northeast Pennsylvania. After your stroll, head down the road to Endless Brewing where you'll feel like family in the cozy taproom.**

Salt Springs State Park is tucked into the Endless Mountains of Northeast Pennsylvania, just shy of the New York border. This easy trail loops through old-growth hemlock forests and along a shallow gorge carved by Fall Brook. Salt Springs State Park is the only Pennsylvania state park managed by a nonprofit, the Friends of Salt Springs. Offering 15 miles of trails, the park is an excellent spot for spotting birds and wildlife.

The Wheaton Family previously owned and operated a dairy farm on the land and their former homestead now functions as a gift shop, office, and historical and environmental center. The park's name refers to the mineral springs that brought Native Americans and settlers alike to the area for the precious salt it produced. Today, the park is popular with locals looking to cool off in the brook, but still flies under the radar for most tourists. This means you may get the peaceful fields and woodlands all to yourself.

From the Gorge Trailhead directly behind Wheaton House, you'll set out on a narrow dirt path. Within the first quarter-mile, you'll crest a hill and see the first two wide waterfalls cascading over rocks down in the gorge. If you're feeling adventurous, you can follow a spur trail down to the water for a stunning close-up view of the first waterfall. Passing the two falls, you'll continue through wetlands and open fields for around half a mile until heading back into the woods on the other side of the brook. The gorge is much higher on this side and enters into

the old-growth hemlock woods that managed to survive the logging boom of the early 1900s. Some of the trees in this area are estimated to be between 300 and 500 years old. Around a mile and a half into the hike at the boardwalk section, you'll get a glimpse of the final waterfall below, similar to the first two but slightly smaller. Just before crossing the bridge back to Wheaton House you'll see the eponymous salt spring.

## TURN-BY-TURN DIRECTIONS

1. From the Park Office at Wheaton House, cross Salt Springs Road to find the blue-blazed Gorge Trail and head uphill on the trail.
2. At 0.1 miles, reach the top of the steep hill.
3. At 0.2 miles, pass a waterfall visible to the left (To the left is an unmarked spur trail down to the falls).
4. At 0.4, cross over Buckley Road and continue straight. Here, the trail becomes the Wetland Trail.
5. At 0.8 miles, keep left at the junction to stay on the Wetland Trail.
6. At 0.9 miles, cross the stream using stepping stones. Just a few feet ahead is another, much smaller stream crossing. Directly after the second stream crossing, keep left to get on the red-blazed Fall Brook Trail.
7. At 1.2 miles, turn left at the junction to stay on the Fall Brook Trail.
8. At 1.3 miles, turn left again, then carefully cross Buckley Road and continue straight on the Fall Brook Trail.
9. At 1.5 miles, after a small stream crossing, head directly uphill on the white-blazed Hemlock Trail. At the top of the hill is a bench to enjoy the view.
10. At 1.6 miles, begin on the boardwalk to the gorge overlook.
11. At 1.8 miles, turn left at the junction to stay on the Hemlock Trail. Follow the trail down the hill.
12. At 1.9 miles, after a sharp left turn, find the salt spring for which the park is named immediately to the left. From here, cross the bridge and the Park Office will be directly ahead.

## FIND THE TRAILHEAD

From Montrose, head north on Route 29. After 5 miles, turn right onto Silver Creek Road. After 1.2 miles, turn left onto Salt Springs Road to access the state park, marked by a large yellow and brown sign. Cross the bridge and the parking lot will be on the right near the barn. The hike begins behind a large white farmhouse called the Wheaton House.

## ENDLESS BREWING

Endless Brewing embraces the pace of slowing down. There's no wifi in this pub, just new friends. Located just down the road from Salt Springs State Park, the cozy indoor taproom offers a small but mighty tap list for thirsty hikers. When the weather cooperates, the taproom spills out into an inviting beer garden that feels like having a beer in a friend's backyard.

Co-owners Morgan Kelly and Jon Winans have been homebrewing since 2007 and officially opened their brewery in 2012. Surrounded by the rolling Endless Mountains for which the brewery is named, Jon built the taproom and brewing facility on his family's farmland. Years before opening the brewery, Jon and Morgan experimented with brewing small batches in a basement. When the community began wanting to buy growlers, they knew this could be the real deal. An unexpected layoff at Jon's work paved the way for starting to brew full-time. Alongside a varied taplist that typically includes IPAs, a cider, and a malty beer, the cozy brewery also includes a rotating menu of daily food specials. Particular favorites include the "Sunday Funday" brunch specials and grilled cheese of the day. The Grasshopper Pale Ale is one of the brewery's original pours; it was on tap the day the brewery opened and has remained a delicious staple on their taplist over the last decade. The bitter crispness of the brew pairs wonderfully with watching the sunset from the brewery's garden.

## LAND MANAGER

**Friends of Salt Springs State Park**
PO Box 541
Montrose, PA 18801
(570) 967-7275
www.friendsofsaltspringspark.org
Map: elibrary.dcnr.pa.gov/GetDocument?docId=1737261&DocName=SALT_ParkMap.pdf

## BREWERY/RESTAURANT

**Endless Brewing**
20610 PA-29
Montrose, PA 18801
(570) 967 0985
www.facebook.com/endlessbrewing

Distance from trailhead: 1.2 miles

# RICKETTS GLEN STATE PARK

## TWENTY-ONE WATERFALLS IN FOUR MILES

| | |
|---|---|
| STARTING POINT | DESTINATION |
| LAKE ROSE TRAILHEAD | THE GLENS NATURAL AREA |
| BREWERY | HIKE TYPE |
| FIVE MOUNTAIN BREWING COMPANY | MODERATE |
| DOG-FRIENDLY | SEASON |
| YES (LEASH REQUIRED) | APRIL–NOVEMBER |
| FEES | DURATION |
| NONE | 2 HOURS 30 MIN. |
| MAP REFERENCE | LENGTH |
| POSTED AT TRAILHEAD | 4.1 MILES (ROUND TRIP) |
| HIGHLIGHTS | ELEVATION GAIN |
| 21 WATERFALLS, ROCK FORMATIONS | 870 FEET |

**6.4 %**
ALCOHOL CONTENT

## BRAASCH FARM-HOUSE SAISON

GOLDEN

CLOVES

CRISP, HERBAL

**BITTERNESS**

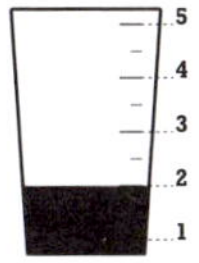


**SWEETNESS**

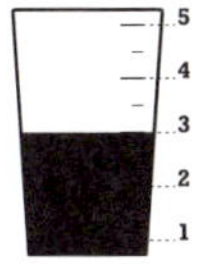


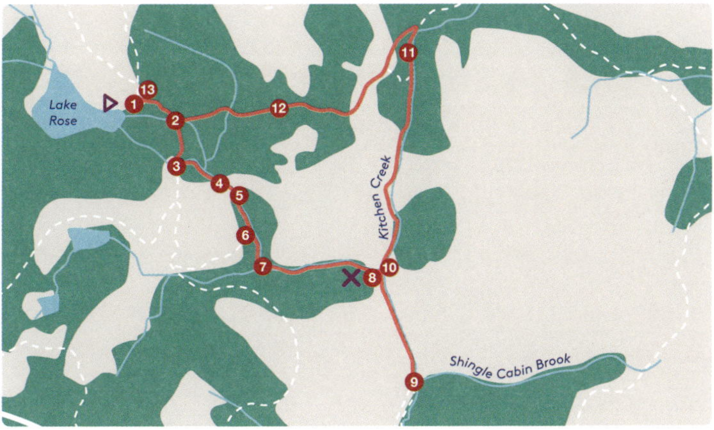


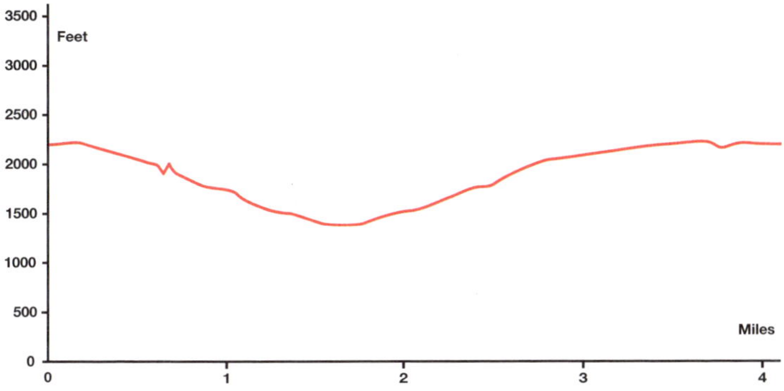

# HIKE DESCRIPTION

**Explore one of Pennsylvania's most breathtaking areas and see twenty-one waterfalls, including the 94-foot Ganoga Falls. Afterward, head into the small town of Shickshinny for a hometown brew at Five Mountain Brewing.**

Ricketts Glen is one of Pennsylvania's greatest gems. It covers over 13,000 acres in Northeastern Pennsylvania, and the section of the park containing the waterfalls is a National Natural Landmark. Although the park is open year-round, you'll get the best results going spring through fall because the trails become treacherously icy in the winter and you'd need proper ice climbing gear to access them.

The park is named for Colonel R. Bruce Ricketts, who bought the land for logging but opted to preserve the extraordinary landscape instead. World War II abruptly ended plans to make the area a National Park, so it has operated as a state park since the 1940s.

Our hike begins on the Highland Trail from the Lake Rose parking lot. Note that this lot can fill up quickly in the summer and on weekends, so plan accordingly (as a backup, you can use the Evergreen parking lot, but this adds about two and a half miles). In around 500 feet, you'll diverge from the Highland Trail and onto the Falls Trail. The majority of the waterfalls in the Glens Natural Area are found along two branches of Kitchen Creek. You'll start out in the Ganoga Glen along the western branch of the creek. The varied terrain can be challenging, but the plethora of cascading falls around each bend will be sure to keep your spirits up. Only 0.5 miles into the trek, you'll reach 94-feet Ganoga Falls, the tallest waterfall in the park. Many of the named waterfalls in the park pay homage to the Susquehannock and Lenape peoples that once lived on the land. After traversing down stone staircases and over bridges for another half-mile, you'll come to Water's Meet where two creek branches meet. Following the trail downstream, you'll pass an additional three waterfalls. Then, you'll return to Water's Meet and follow the eastern branch of Kitchen Creek into Glen Leigh. Now, you'll be traveling uphill alongside the creek and waterfalls. After passing the final waterfall, you'll turn left to leave the Falls Trail. A quick jaunt on the Highland Trail connects the two sides of the Glen and leads back to the parking lot, passing through a crevasse in two large sandstone blocks.

## TURN-BY-TURN DIRECTIONS

1. From the Lake Rose parking lot, take the trail next to the map kiosk.
2. At 0.1 miles, turn right to stay on the signposted Falls Trail.
3. At 0.3 miles, cross a small bridge and turn left at a junction to remain on the signposted Falls Trail. The first waterfall will be to the left.
4. At 0.5 miles, view Oneida Falls to the left.
5. At 0.6 miles, go down the steps and see Cayuga Falls to the left.
6. At 0.7 miles, continue straight on the Falls Trail which twists down the hillside. Ganoga Falls will be visible after the first bend.
7. At 0.8 miles, cross a small bridge and continue along the trail.
8. At 1.3 miles, after passing several more waterfalls, reach an intersection and continue straight on the Falls Trail.
9. At 1.6 miles, reach the Murray Reynolds waterfall. Here, turn around and retrace your steps along the Falls Trail back to the intersection from step 8.
10. At 1.9 miles, at the intersection from step 8, turn right and cross the bridge to enter the Glen Leigh section of the trail.
11. At 2.9 miles, view Onondaga Falls to the right, the last falls on the loop. Just after passing the falls, turn left onto the Highland Trail.
12. At 3.6 miles, pass through the Midway Crevasse, a unique geological feature.
13. At 4.1 miles, complete the loop and return to the parking lot.

## FIND THE TRAILHEAD

From PA-487 in Red Rock, turn left by the Red Rock Corner Store in Benton to stay on PA-487. After 3.7 miles, turn left into Ricketts Glen State Park. Pass the park office and stay on the main road. In 0.4 miles, turn right following signs for Lake Rose trailhead. Continue on this narrow road for 0.6 miles, which ends at the trailhead. Only park in designated spots in the lot.

# FIVE MOUNTAIN BREWING COMPANY

Five Mountain Brewery is tucked into the quaint town of Shickshinny. Taking its name from the five mountains that surround the town, the brewery has been a hometown staple since it opened its doors in 2018. Like many brewery owners, Melissa and Brent Humm dabbled in homebrewing and grew their brewing capacity from there. Knowing they wanted to open a small business, they eventually found a small space to open a modest taproom. It was such a small operation that the first kegs were made on their original homebrew equipment! The team moved to the current location in 2021, which features an outdoor patio and a larger space, which allows them to host their popular comedy nights. Despite the larger space, the Humms still make the taproom feel like a cozy living room, with games for kids, a fireplace, and a wall of personalized mugs for the locals.

The Braasch Farmhouse Ale is a loving nod to the legacy of the owner's family and the memories of their dairy farm. While enjoying a brew in the cozy taproom, be sure to check out their restaurant menu for something comforting to chow on. The bangers and mash pair particularly well with the Braasch Farmhouse!

## LAND MANAGER

**Ricketts Glen State Park**
PA Dept of Conservation and Natural Resources
695 State Route 487
Benton, PA 17814
(570) 477-5675
www.dcnr.pa.gov/StateParks/FindAPark/RickettsGlenStatePark
Map: elibrary.dcnr.pa.gov/GetDocument?docId=1753204&DocName=RICK_GlensMap.pdf

## BREWERY/RESTAURANT

**Five Mountain Brewing Company**
22 Main Street
Shickshinny, PA 18655
www.fivemountainbeer.com

Distance from trailhead: 19 miles

# SHADES OF DEATH

## A SINISTER NAME FOR AN INVITING CREEKSIDE RAMBLE

| STARTING POINT | DESTINATION |
|---|---|
| HICKORY RUN STATE PARK OFFICE | SHADES OF DEATH TRAIL |
| **BREWERY** | **HIKE TYPE** |
| BRIGHT PATH BREWING | MODERATE |
| **DOG-FRIENDLY** | **SEASON** |
| YES (LEASH REQUIRED) | YEAR-ROUND |
| **FEES** | **DURATION** |
| NONE | 1 HOUR 30 MIN. |
| **MAP REFERENCE** | **LENGTH** |
| POSTED ON PARK OFFICE BULLETIN | 2.6 MILES (ROUND TRIP) |
| **HIGHLIGHTS** | **ELEVATION GAIN** |
| WATERFALLS, DAM LOCKS, BOULDER SQUEEZE | 370 FEET |

4.5 %
ALCOHOL CONTENT

AMERICAN STANDARD PALE ALE

YELLOW

LIGHT

BRIGHT, CITRUS

BITTERNESS

SWEETNESS

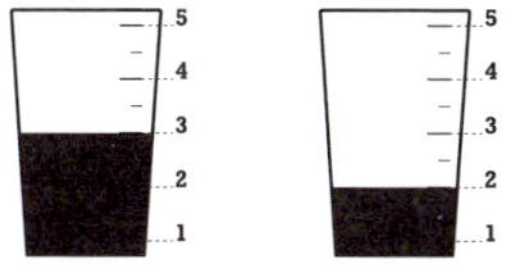


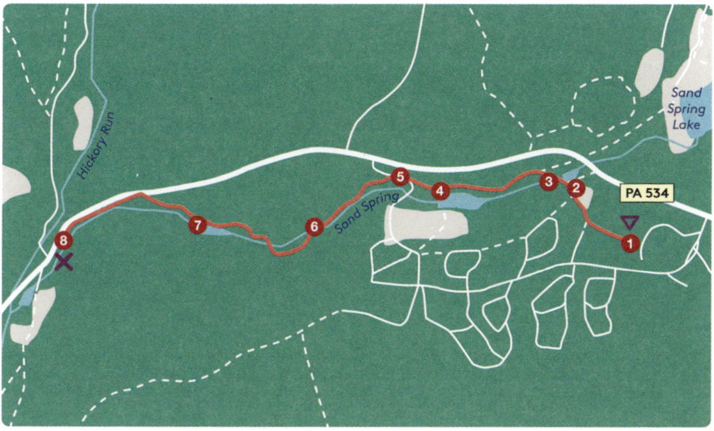


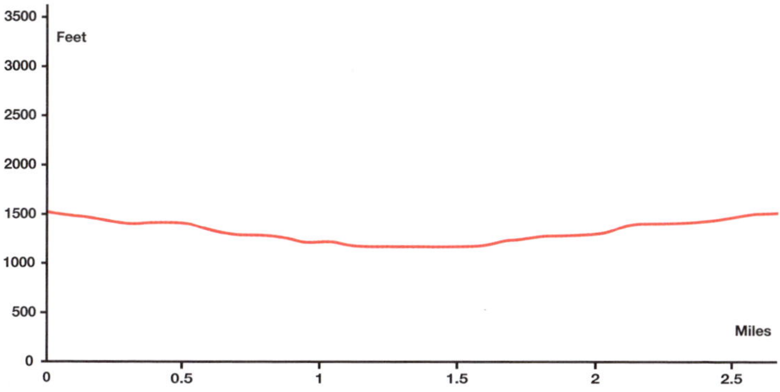

# HIKE DESCRIPTION

**Take this ominously named hike along a creek featuring several waterfall dams. Afterward, have a brew at Bright Path Brewing in the quaint town of Jim Thorpe, touted as the resting place of the famed athlete.**

Hickory Run State Park is a large park nestled in the Poconos Mountains in Carbon County, Pennsylvania. In addition to over 40 miles of hiking trails, this park is a popular spot for a variety of recreational activities including swimming, camping, and fishing. It's best known for the geologically unique Boulder Field, a National Natural Landmark. Although the park is quite popular, you can still find solitude along the trails, especially when visiting on weekdays or off-season.

The Shades of Death Trail is a moderately difficult trail that travels through dense rhododendron thickets along the Sand Spring Run stream. While the name Shades of Death may be chilling, it refers to the nickname that early settlers gave the area because of the shadowy forests, rocky terrain, and poor soil, thus making it "deadly" for farming. In reality, the trail is incredibly picturesque, with dappled sunlight falling on the water spilling from dams along the stream.

There are two access points to the trail, but the easiest one is at the large visitor center with ample parking. To get to the Shades of Death Trail, you'll follow the paved path behind the building. It's easy to then

follow the trail out and back as it hugs close to Sandy Springs Run. Along the trail, you'll enjoy stunning views of the water as it tumbles over two man-made dams built by the Civilian Conservation Corps in the 1930s. A little over three-quarters of a mile into your trek, you'll cross a small boulder field with some technical scrambles over rocks. Then you'll squeeze through a narrow crevice between two large boulders before returning to the streamside trail. This hike stays green all year round as it passes through dense hemlock woods that have regrown in the years following the logging boom of the mid-1800s. Hemlock trees were prized for the acid tannin in their bark, a key ingredient in the tanning process. After passing alongside the stream for just over a mile, you'll emerge into a parking lot where you'll turn around and enjoy the Shades of Death all over again.

## TURN-BY-TURN DIRECTIONS

1. The trail starts on the paved path behind the visitor center.
2. At 0.2 miles, leave the paved trail to turn left down the hill on an unmarked trail.
3. At 0.3 miles, cross the bridge over the stream, then turn left onto the Shades of Death Trail, marked by yellow paint on trees and rocks.
4. At 0.5 miles, turn right to walk through the field.
5. At 0.6 miles, at the trail sign for Shades of Death, turn left to cross over the campground road, following along the gravel path and down the stairs.
6. At 0.8 miles, cross through a small boulder field and then pass through a rock crevice. Look for the trail markers on rocks.
7. At 1.0 miles, pass a waterfall from the dam on the left.
8. At 1.3 miles, the trail lets out into a parking lot. Turn around and return on the same path.

## FIND THE TRAILHEAD

From I-80E in White Haven, take Exit 274 for PA-534E. At the end of the off-ramp, turn right onto PA-534; proceed for 1.8 miles. At the stop sign, turn left to stay on PA-534. After 4.6 miles, turn right onto Family Camp Road, by the campground sign. The visitor center parking lot is immediately to the right. The trail begins behind the visitor center on the paved path.

# BRIGHT PATH BREWING

Tucked into the southwest corner of the Pocono Mountains is the quaint town of Jim Thorpe, Pennsylvania, named for the famous Native American athlete. Popular for outdoor recreation and scenic views, Bright Path Brewing is an essential highlight of the region. According to co-owner and brewer Dillon Smith, Jim Thorpe, of the Sac and Fox Nation, was called Wa-Tho-Huk in his native tongue which translates to Bright Path in English. Smith and his business partner Alex Franko wanted to pay homage to the famed athlete and thus, Bright Path Brewing was born. Smith and Franko both worked at breweries across the East Coast before bringing their expertise back to their hometown. Since opening in 2021, Bright Path has focused on low ABV lagers and session ales and exudes a community-forward ambience. This is a taproom made for easy-drinking and a pour of the fittingly named American Standard fits the bill.

Uniquely filling from a side pull, also called a Czech beer faucet, this pale ale has a light citrus taste and is thirst-quenching after a day out on the trails. Both brewers are outdoor enthusiasts so many of the beer names give a nod to the great outdoors in the Poconos region.

## LAND MANAGER

**Hickory Run State Park**
3 Family Camp Road
White Haven, PA 18661
(272) 808-6192
www.dcnr.pa.gov/StateParks/FindAPark/HickoryRunStatePark
Map: elibrary.dcnr.pa.gov/GetDocument?docId=1737640&DocName=HICK_ParkMap.pdf

## BREWERY/RESTAURANT

**Bright Path Brewery**
1215 North Street
Jim Thorpe, PA 18229
(570) 732-9990
www.brightpathbrewing.com

Distance from trailhead: 17 miles

# HAWK MOUNTAIN

## VIEW RAPTORS AT THIS STUNNING OVERLOOK

| STARTING POINT | DESTINATION |
|---|---|
| NATIVE HABITAT GARDEN | NORTH LOOKOUT |
| BREWERY | HIKE TYPE |
| THE REFEREND BIER BLENDERY | STRENUOUS |
| DOG-FRIENDLY | SEASON |
| NO | YEAR-ROUND |
| FEES | DURATION |
| YES | 3 HOURS |
| MAP REFERENCE | LENGTH |
| ALLTRAILS | 5 MILES (LOOP) |
| HIGHLIGHTS | ELEVATION GAIN |
| ROCK SCRAMBLE, BOULDER FIELD, WILDLIFE | 1,050 FEET |

**6.9%** ALCOHOL CONTENT

## KRAK! GOLDEN ALE

RUBY

RIPE CHERRIES

EARTHY, TART

BITTERNESS

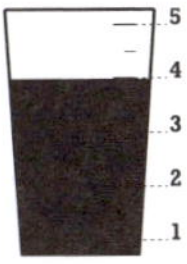


SWEETNESS

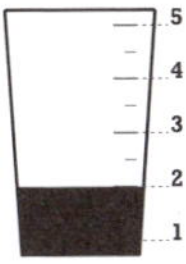


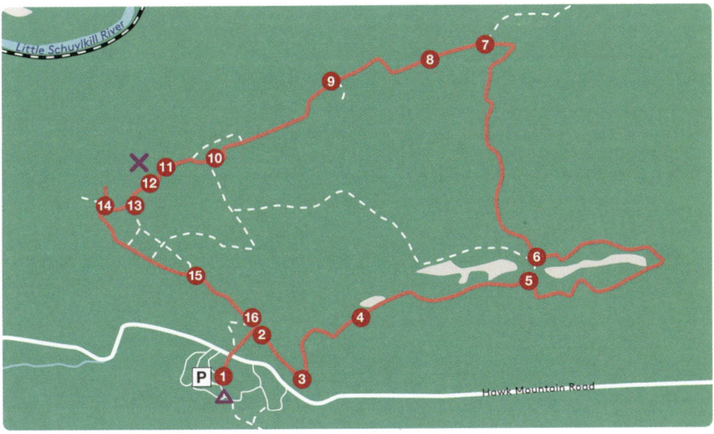


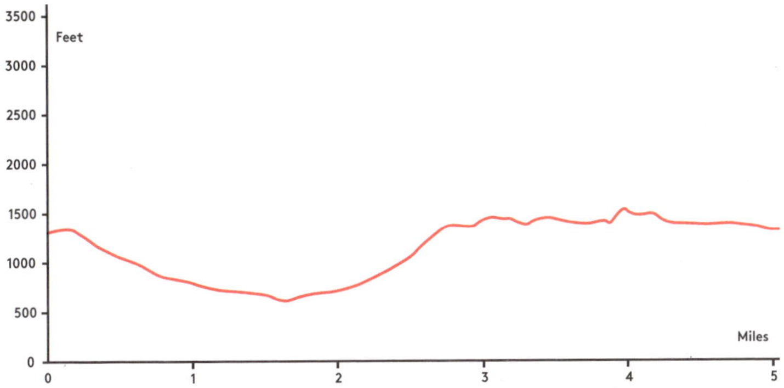

# HIKE DESCRIPTION

**The chance to see soaring birds of prey is your reward for conquering challenging rock scrambles at Hawk Mountain Sanctuary. Post-hike, toast your success at the Referend Bier Blendery, which specializes in spontaneously fermented beer.**

Hawk Mountain Sanctuary is a nonprofit wild bird preserve for conservation and public education about raptors. There is a modest fee for using the hiking trails which supports sanctuary stewardship and trail maintenance. Buy a trail pass online or in the visitor center before setting out.

This loop tackles some of the most challenging trails in the Sanctuary. The first section follows the red-blazed River of Rocks trail, which passes beside boulder tracts along a rock-covered trail. The trail runs alongside a large boulder field that sits atop an underground stream, appearing like a wide river of stone. After two miles traversing the rugged path, you'll be onto the next challenge: The Golden Eagle Trail.

The yellow-blazed trail ascends over 600 feet in under a mile. It is far less rocky, but the steep grade presents a challenging climb. After cresting the top, you'll join the blue-blazed Skyline Trail. However, this is no easy stroll along a ridge. The trail becomes rocky once again and some spots need hands and feet to clamber up the rocks!

After a final push up a 30-foot rock pile, you'll reach the stunning expanse of North Lookout. The overlook offers 200° views and is the best spot for viewing raptors like bald eagles, turkey vultures, Cooper's hawks, Northern Goshawk, and many more. A hundred years ago, hunters filled this overlook, shooting hundreds a day because they believed raptors were a menace. In 1934, conservationist Rosalie Edge leased the land and opened it as a space for tracking wild birds and educating the public about their importance. Now, nature lovers flock to the mountain to watch the birds soar along their natural highways in the sky. During migration periods (April-May and Sept-Nov), the Sanctuary sees nearly 20,000 birds of prey.

After enjoying the views and soaring birds, continue along the ridge, heading toward the trees. You'll now be on the orange-blazed Lookout Trail, from which you'll get several viewpoints, although none quite as majestic as the North Lookout. One viewpoint, accessed via a short out-and-back, is known as The Slide. Before the Sanctuary was established, people quarried sandstone at the mountain. With no easy way to transport the stone back down the hillside, they crafted a pulley cable car system. You can still see the foundation of the old brake house at the Slide point.

Finally, you'll finish your hike with a gentle descent along the Lookout Trail to the final vista. At nearly 5 miles, you'll reach South Lookout, the final vista where you finish your loop of Hawk Mountain. After savoring your last look at the valley below, head down the paved path toward the Sanctuary entrance.

## TURN-BY-TURN DIRECTIONS

1. Start on the paved trail outside the gates for the Native Habitat Garden. Carefully cross the road and pass the welcome station and then continue uphill on the wide path.
2. At 0.2 miles, turn right onto the red-blazed River of Rocks Trail. The trail is marked with a large brown sign and a rock pedestal with information about wildlife.
3. At 0.3 miles, cross through a small boulder field on the River of Rocks Trail.
4. At 0.6 miles, there is a large rock field to the left of the trail.
5. At 1.2 miles, turn right on the River of Rocks Trail. In 200 feet, turn left to stay on the River of Rocks Trail.
6. At 2.0 miles, turn right at the four-way intersection to get on the yellow-blazed Golden Eagle Trail.
7. At 2.8 miles, reach the top of the hill where the Golden Eagle Trail meets with the blue-blazed Skyline Trail. Turn left and follow the yellow/blue trail.

8. At 3.0 miles, there is a rocky uphill scramble.
9. At 3.3 miles, there is an optional side trail to the East Rocks viewpoint (not included in this official route mileage).
10. At 3.7 miles, at the T-intersection where the Skyline Trail splits from the Golden Eagle Trail, turn right to stay on the Skyline Trail.
11. At 3.8 miles, there is a steep rock scramble up a hillside.
12. At 3.9 miles, reach North Lookout. After leaving the overlook, begin to follow the orange-blazed Lookout Trail.
13. At 4.0 miles, head down the stairs. Continue straight along the Lookout Trail.
14. At 4.1 miles, turn right at the four-way intersection to follow signs to The Slide overlook. Once you've reached The Slide overlook return to the intersection and head down the stairs.
15. At 4.5 miles, Bald Lookout is to the left. Continue along the Orange Trail, passing several other small vistas.
16. At 4.8 miles, reach South Lookout, the final vista on the hike. Turn right to return to the parking lot on the paved path.

## FIND THE TRAILHEAD

From I-78 in Hamburg, take Exit 29B for N. PA-61. At the end of the ramp, use the right lane to merge onto N. PA-61; proceed for 4.1 miles. At the traffic light, turn right onto E. PA-895. In 1.5 miles, turn right onto Hawk Mountain Road. After 0.5 miles, turn right into the gravel parking lot for the visitor center, marked by a large brown sign. To start the hike, begin on the paved path outside of the large gate for the Native Habitat Garden.

## THE REFEREND BIER BLENDERY

A wild ale is a special type of beer brewed using only naturally occurring yeast, a process known as spontaneous fermentation. Brewer's yeast ferments most beers, but a wild ale relies solely on the bacteria in the environment. Think sourdough, but with beer. That's exactly the style that James Priest and his wife Melissa Ducommun Priest have spent years perfecting. James became fascinated with wild ales while working at breweries and wineries for five years. In 2016, James struck out with Melissa to tap into the world of wild ales and opened Referend Bier Blendery. In the beginning, the Blendery taproom and barrel cellar were based in Central NJ. With no brewing equipment of their own, they borrowed time on other breweries' equipment to brew the wort. Then, they acclimatized it in a coolship in the back of a Budget truck. Back at the cellar, they added the cooled wort to barrels and let it age for at least six months and up to four years. If there's one thing Referend has perfected, it's patience.

Now at their farm in Pennsylvania where they've been since 2021, Referend brews and blends on-site. Located on a former winery with established orchards and gardens, the move also further empowered the owners to source all regional grain and fruits for their brews. Krak! is a golden ale re-fermented on New York sour cherries. A Kriek Lambic is a traditional type of Belgian wild ale fermented on sour cherries, hence the beer's name. Krak! undergoes an eighteen-month fermenting and aging process before bottling. Its complex cherry flavor is best savored slowly.

### LAND MANAGER

**Hawk Mountain Sanctuary**
1700 Hawk Mountain Road
Kempton, PA 19529
(610) 756-6961
www.hawkmountain.org
Map: www.hawkmountain.org/visit/hiking/trail-descriptions

### BREWERY/RESTAURANT

**The Referend Bier Blendery**
407 Old U.S. 22,
Kutztown, PA 19530
(609) 474-0443
www.thereferend.com

Distance from trailhead: 13 miles

# KELLYS RUN

## CREEK CASCADES IN THE HEART OF AMISH COUNTRY

| STARTING POINT | DESTINATION |
|---|---|
| OLD HOLTWOOD ROAD PAVILION | KELLYS RUN |
| BREWERY | HIKE TYPE |
| SOUTH COUNTY BREWING CO. | MODERATE |
| DOG-FRIENDLY | SEASON |
| YES (LEASH REQUIRED) | YEAR-ROUND |
| FEES | DURATION |
| NONE | 1 HOUR 30 MIN. |
| MAP REFERENCE | LENGTH |
| KELLYS RUN & HOLTWOOD PRESERVE BROCHURE | 3.7 MILES (LOOP) |
| HIGHLIGHTS | ELEVATION GAIN |
| CREEK, WILDFLOWERS, ROCK SCRAMBLES | 620 FEET |

**5.0 %**
**ALCOHOL CONTENT**

## ASTRAL DRIFT HAZY PALE ALE

**CLOUDY YELLOW**

**FRUITY**

**SUMMER MELON**

**BITTERNESS**

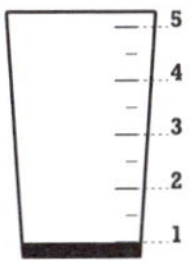


**SWEETNESS**

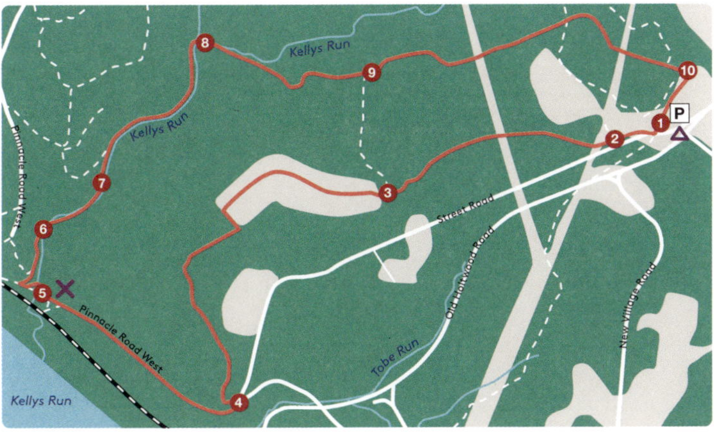


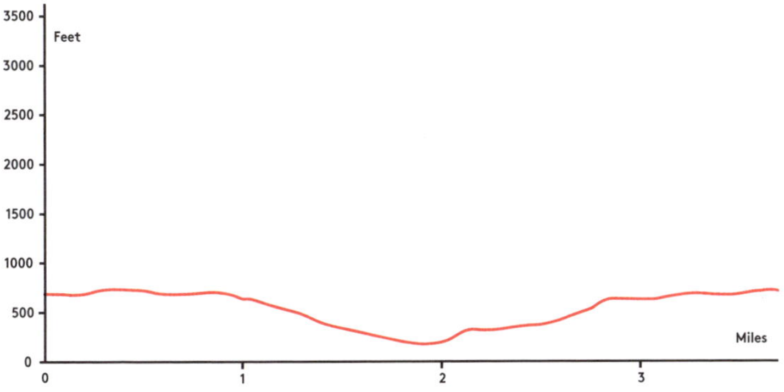

# HIKE DESCRIPTION

**Follow this trail through a jungle of ferns and rhododendron bushes as you pass along a creek spilling over rocks and boulders. Later, relax on the sunny patio at South Country Brewing.**

From grassy wildflower fields to rock scrambles over a stream, Kellys Run Nature Preserve is full of adventure. Maintained by the Lancaster Conservancy, the nature preserve makes up 450 acres of protected land managed for recreation. Directly to the south is the Holtwood Nature Preserve, which provides a safe space for habitat restoration.

Tucked into the heart of Amish country, Kellys Run is a charming break in the Lancaster County farmland. The hike begins at the preserve's main parking lot where you'll find ample parking, restrooms, a large picnic pavilion, and a kiosk with a trail map. The entire loop follows the blue-blazed Kellys Run Trail, which begins to the left of the pavilion along a grassy path. As you start the trail, notice the pollinator park to the right filled with meadow grasses and wildflowers. This volunteer initiative by Lancaster Conservancy reclaimed 14 acres of abandoned parkland coinciding with an electric utility line and transformed it into a bird and pollinator habitat. They've also worked with local farmers to introduce native bees into the habitat to serve for honey production and pollination for regional farms.

You'll continue along the Kellys Run Trail as it heads into a shady stretch full of tall trees and vine-covered underbrush. The trail then opens up into a large meadow with a mown trail lined with grasses and milkweed. This is a butterfly paradise in the summer, and you may even spot monarch butterflies feeding on their favorite snack:

milkweed nectar. This is also a fantastic spot for birdwatching as songbird species like goldfinches love to feed on the seeds of wildflowers and tall grasses.

As the path leaves the meadow and starts on a steep descent, tall hardwood trees surround you. After about a half mile, you'll reach another small parking lot with room for only a few cars. To the left, through breaks in the trees, you'll see the Susquehanna River below. You might also hear the distant sounds of the railroad that follows alongside the river. After following a narrow road for less than a mile, you'll see the remains of an old metal bridge from the days when this was a functioning road. The bridge is in poor shape, so don't cross here. Instead, follow the trail to the right and use the stepping stones to hop across the small stream known as Kellys Run.

At this point, you've reached the Kellys Run Gorge and the landscape becomes markedly different. Suddenly, you're in a world of ferns, moss-covered boulders, and small cascades as the stream tumbles its way down to join the Susquehanna River. For the next mile, the trail meanders alongside and over the stream for some of the most beautiful landscapes that Lancaster County has to offer. While the hike up to this point is fairly easy, this section can be quite challenging, with frequent rock scrambles and stream crossings. During the spring and after heavy rains, the cascades will be more pronounced, and you'll likely get wet while crossing. This section is particularly stunning in the early summer when the rhododendron and mountain laurels lining the stream burst into bloom. The shaded dampness also makes Kellys Run a prime spot for wildflowers like Jack-in-the-pulpit and wild geranium, as well as amphibians like salamanders and newts.

After a mile, the Kellys Run Trail eventually starts its ascent, leaving the magnificent gorge behind. You'll continue along a steep cliff covered with moss and ferns before emerging into peaceful woods of maple and oak trees. Finally you'll head into an open grassy field and continue along the path until the pavilion and parking lot reappear ahead.

# TURN-BY-TURN DIRECTIONS

1. From the parking lot, follow the Kellys Run Trail to the left of the pavilion marked by blue blazes on tree trunks.
2. At 0.1 miles, continue straight at the T-junction.
3. At 0.6 miles, continue straight on the blue-blazed Kellys Run Trail.
4. At 1.4 miles, reach a parking lot. Make a sharp right turn onto the narrow paved road.
5. At 1.8 miles, turn right off the paved trail and use the stones to cross Kellys Run. After crossing, turn right up the hill.
6. At 2.0 miles, use the stones to cross Kellys Run again.
7. At 2.2 miles, cross back over the stream. Afterward, turn right at the Y-junction to stay on the blue-blazed Kellys Run Trail.
8. At 2.5 miles, cross an unnamed stream that joins with Kellys Run and then turn right to stay on the Kellys Run Trail.
9. At 2.9 miles, continue straight at the junction to stay on the Kellys Run Trail.
10. At 3.6 miles, turn right into the field and head toward the pavilion and parking lot.

# FIND THE TRAILHEAD

From Lancaster, head south on US-222. After 3 miles, the road continues straight and becomes US-272/Lancaster Pike. After 9 miles, use the right lane to exit onto US-372/Holtwood Road. Continue for 5 miles before turning right onto River Road. After 0.5 miles, turn left onto Old Holtwood Road. After 0.7 miles, bear right at the fork onto Street Road. The park entrance will be to the right about 400 feet ahead. There is no sign at the entrance, but there will be a large pavilion and wooden trailhead kiosk beside it.

# SOUTH COUNTY BREWING

South County Brewing has its humble origins in Fawn Grove, Pennsylvania, where owner and head brewer JR Heaps launched his taproom back in 2011, setting up shop next door to his brother's auto body shop. After losing his job working in historic restoration during the 2008 recession, JR took the opportunity to pivot toward brewing. What had been a hobby became a new opportunity, and JR took a leap of faith to attend brewery school in Chicago. With his newly-honed skills, he built the whole brewing system for his new taproom by hand and even sold beer from his car to get the brand up and running.

Fast forward to today, JR and new co-owner Sam Tessero have a new destination brewery location in York on 13 acres of land. The new facility is part modern brewing facility and part oaken cathedral, complete with vaulted ceilings of wooden beams supporting Amish-made chandeliers and light fixtures. Outside is a large stone patio complete with adirondack chairs and firepits. The original Fawn Grove space remains as a retail taproom only.

Along with a menu of pizza, BBQ, and entrees, the tap list offers a range of experimental flavors and classics. The Astral Drift is a thirst-quenching pale ale perfect for sipping while soaking in the sun.

## LAND MANAGER

**Lancaster Conservancy**
117 S. West End Avenue
Lancaster, PA 17603
(717) 392-7891
www.lancasterconservancy.org
Map: www.lancasterconservancy.org/preserves/kellys-run

## BREWERY/RESTAURANT

**South County Brewing**
170 Crossway Drive, York, PA 17402
(717) 714-5270
www.southcountybrewing.com

Distance from trailhead: 25 miles

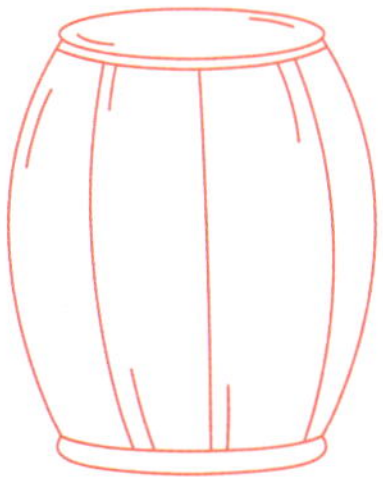

# HIGH ROCKS VISTA

## ROCKY VIEWS ON A CREEKSIDE TRAIL

| STARTING POINT | DESTINATION |
|---|---|
| TOHICKON VALLEY PARKING LOT | HIGH ROCKS VISTA |
| **BREWERY** | **HIKE TYPE** |
| WARWICK FARM BREWING | MODERATE |
| **DOG-FRIENDLY** | **SEASON** |
| YES (LEASH REQUIRED) | YEAR-ROUND |
| **FEES** | **DURATION** |
| NONE | 1 HOUR 30 MIN. |
| **MAP REFERENCE** | **LENGTH** |
| ALL TRAILS | 3.5 MILES (LOOP) |
| **HIGHLIGHTS** | **ELEVATION GAIN** |
| ROCKY OUTCROPPING, CREEK | 423 FEET |

5.2 %
ALCOHOL CONTENT

## WARWICK WIT

CLOUDY GOLD

ORANGE, BLACK PEPPER

WHEAT, CORIANDER

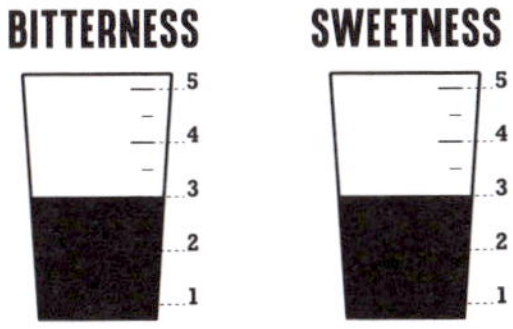


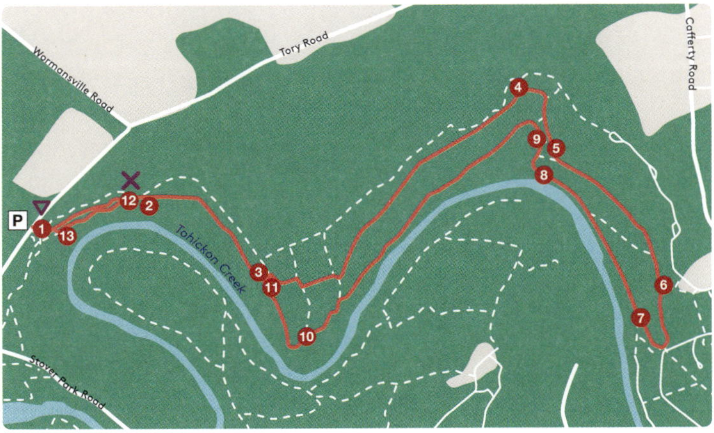


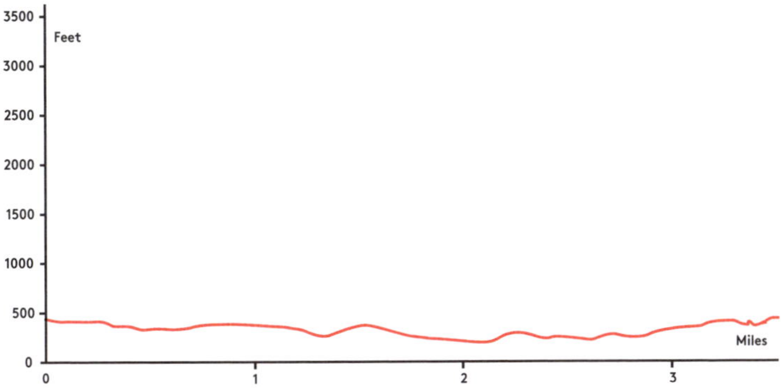

# HIKE DESCRIPTION

**Hike along the jagged High Rocks Vista to see a dramatic horseshoe bend in Tohickon Creek. Afterward, head to the sprawling Warwick Farm Brewing for a draft at a working hop farm.**

The High Rocks Vista area is a popular trail system passing through Ralph Stover State Park and Tohickon Valley Park (managed by Bucks County Parks and Recreation). Despite its popularity, the meandering trails can be difficult to follow, so it helps to download the route beforehand. Your hike begins on the Yellow Trail, which splits into a lower section along the cliff edge and an upper section in the woods. You can start on either section, but for these directions, you'll want to start along the upper section so you end your hike with stunning cliffside views.

The Yellow Trail meanders along the ridge with glimpses of the Tohickon Gorge and the creek flowing below. Rocks dot the dark red clay soil so you'll want to watch where you step. About a mile in, you'll cross a rocky hillside stream that drains into Tohickon Creek. The Lenni Lenape people called the creek "To-Hick-Hanne" or "Deer-Bone-creek." This 30-mile creek eventually flows into the Delaware River where it becomes an exciting whitewater kayaking spot during times of high water. Keep your eyes out for vibrant kayaks dotting the waters below.

About a mile and a half along the trail, you'll come to a trail intersection with an access trail to the nearby campground. You'll get on the Orange Trail and follow it downhill as it makes a wide bend alongside the creek. Just before you turn to hike back uphill, there is a clearing in the trees along the water; this is a perfect spot to walk down to the creek bed. As you head back up the hillside, you'll notice that the Orange Trail is more rocky than the Yellow Trail. Although you'll be looking down a lot, be sure to glance up and appreciate the surrounding stately maple and beech trees.

After rejoining the Yellow Trail for the final leg of the hike, you'll return to the High Rocks area. You can thank Buck County's most famous author for preserving this geological wonder for generations to come. James A. Michener, the Pulitzer Prize-winning author whose work inspired the classic Broadway hit South Pacific, gifted the land to Bucks County Parks in 1959. Approaching the cliffs, you'll take the lower Yellow Trail to walk along the 150-foot cliffs. These sheer rock walls are popular with experienced rock climbers, but please don't venture beyond the railings for your safety. The final vista is arguably the most impressive with clear views of the creek below. Beautiful at any time of year, it's especially stunning in the winter when the horseshoe bend in the creek is unobstructed by greenery.

## TURN-BY-TURN DIRECTIONS

1. From the parking lot, head straight across the street onto the unmarked dirt trail. In 100 feet, turn left to start on the marked Yellow Trail.
2. At 0.2 miles, to the right, there is a creek vista from the top of the cliffs.
3. At 0.5 miles, reach a Y-junction with the Orange Trail; turn left to continue on the Yellow Trail. Ignore the unmarked access trails to other trail systems.
4. At 1.1 miles, turn right to stay on the Yellow Trail and use the rocks to cross over two small runoff streams.
5. At 1.3 miles, turn left to continue on the Yellow Trail, ignoring the shortcut trails to other paths.
6. At 1.6 miles, turn right to leave the Yellow Trail and begin on the Orange Trail. Do not follow the signs for the campground.
7. At 1.8 miles, stay to the right to continue along the Orange Trail, now following along the creek.
8. At 2.1 miles, there is a convenient break in the trees and a stone path down to the water's edge.
9. At 2.2 miles, turn left to continue on the Orange Trail, ignoring the unmarked trail to the right.
10. At 2.8 miles, turn left on the Orange Trail; then curve around a wide landing overlooking the creek below. The trail now begins to head uphill.
11. At 3.0 miles, make a sharp left at the same Y-junction from Step 3 to return to the Yellow Trail.
12. At 3.3 miles, after passing the same vista from Step 2, take the left path to start on the lower Yellow Trail, following along the cliff's edge for multiple viewpoints from High Rocks.
13. At 3.5 miles, pass the final viewpoint; then turn right to return to the Yellow Trail, which leads back to the parking lot.

## FIND THE TRAILHEAD

From Doylestown, head north on PA-611. Proceed for 7.3 miles; then turn right at the traffic light onto Deep Run Road/Route 413. In 0.2 miles, turn right to remain on Route 413. After another 0.2 miles, when Route 413 crosses over Durham Road, it becomes Dark Hollow Road. Continue on Dark Hollow Road for 2.2 miles; then turn right onto Stover Park Road. Continue on the narrow road for 0.9 miles; then turn left onto Tory Road, a narrow dirt road. The trailhead parking will be on the left in 0.2 miles. The trail begins on the right side of the road, directly across from the parking area. There is no sign for the trail, but there is a trail kiosk with a posted trail map.

# WARWICK FARM BREWING

In a region dominated by wineries, Warwick Farm Brewing is a beer-drinker's dream. In 2018 two father/son duos, Scott and Ryan Seiz and Tom and Tim Tabor, opened the brewery. At the end of his pro-baseball career, Ryan dove headfirst into home brewing. He spent years experimenting and perfecting his recipes with his father, Scott. Eventually, the two tossed around the idea of opening a brewery with family friends, Tom and Tim, who had bought and were working to preserve a 22-acre historic farm. Together, the four hoped to transform it into a destination farm brewery.

The brewery officially opened in 2019, offering crowlers and can sales only. Ryan, head brewer, and Tim, general manager, were blown away by the local community's enthusiasm for their brews. The team worked tirelessly behind the scenes to construct a 5,000-square-foot taproom. Finally opening in 2022, the farm offers a full experience with traditional taproom seating and a sprawling outdoor beer garden overlooking the rolling hills of Bucks County. The Seizes and Tabors use four hop varieties grown on-site in several of their beers. At Warwick Farms, nothing goes to waste. They give their spent grains to other neighboring farms to use as feed or compost them as soil enrichment.

The Warwick Wit is a zesty take on a traditional witbier with fresh orange zest and coriander added to the brew. If purchasing cans, store them upside down as the can directs. This allows the unfiltered yeast to reincorporate into the brew for a more robust flavor.

## LAND MANAGER

**Bucks County Parks & Recreation**
901 E. Bridgetown Pike
Langhorne, PA 19047
(215) 757-0571
www.buckscounty.gov/Facilities/Facility/Details/Tohickon-Valley-Park-8
Map: elibrary.dcnr.pa.gov/GetDocument?docId=1737295&DocName=RAST_ParkMap.pdf

## BREWERY/RESTAURANT

**Warwick Farm Brewing**
800 Almshouse Road
Jamison, PA 18929
(215) 792-7599
www.warwickfarmbrewing.com

Distance from trailhead: 18 miles

# RIDLEY CREEK STATE PARK

**MEANDER PAST AN ENGLISH MANOR IN A LUSH WOODLAND PARK**

| STARTING POINT | DESTINATION |
|---|---|
| STATE PARK OFFICE | RIDLEY CREEK |
| BREWERY | HIKE TYPE |
| LEVANTE BREWING COMPANY | MODERATE |
| DOG-FRIENDLY | SEASON |
| YES (LEASH REQUIRED) | YEAR-ROUND |
| FEES | DURATION |
| NONE | 2 HOURS |
| MAP REFERENCE | LENGTH |
| POSTED AT TRAILHEAD | 4.6 MILES (LOOP) |
| HIGHLIGHTS | ELEVATION GAIN |
| CREEK, WILDFLOWERS, HISTORIC SITES | 614 FEET |

**5.9 %**
ALCOHOL CONTENT

## CLOUDY & CUMBERSOME NEW ENGLAND IPA

OPAQUE ORANGE

TROPICAL FRUIT

BREADY,
TROPICAL

**BITTERNESS**

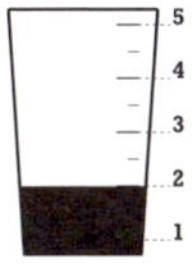


**SWEETNESS**

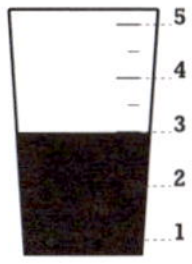


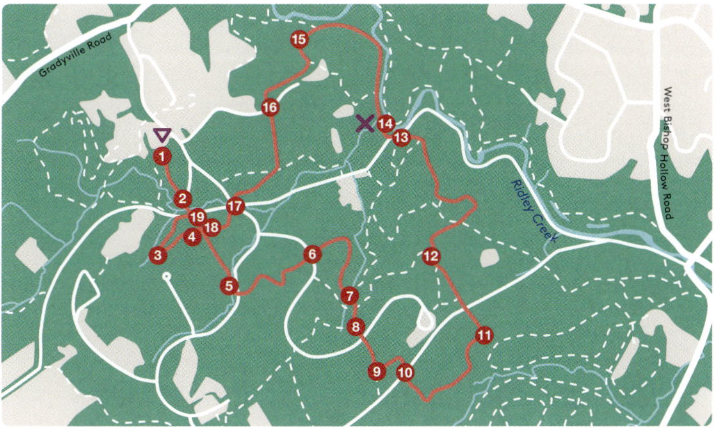


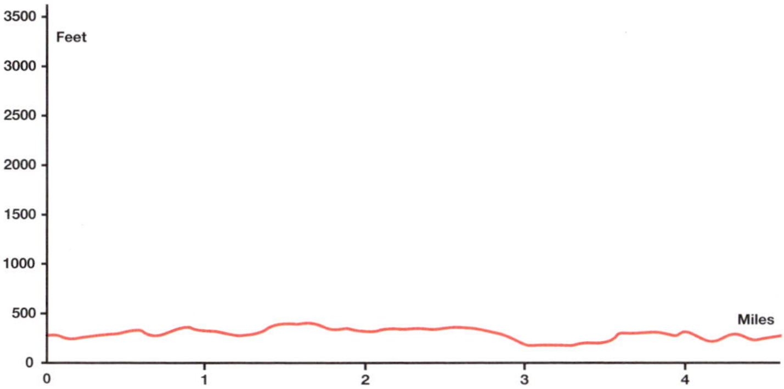

# HIKE DESCRIPTION

**Discover miles of wooded trails only 16 miles away from downtown Philadelphia featuring a historic mansion and creekside paths. Later, roll up to the community-focused Levante Brewing taproom for a tropical patio beer.**

Ridley Creek State Park is a green oasis, encompassing over 2,600 acres of land in Delaware County. Nestled into the sprawling woodlands, it's difficult to imagine that the bustling streets of Philadelphia are only 16 miles away! This park is an outdoor enthusiast's dream, with multi-use trails for bicycling, running, hiking, mountain biking, and horseback riding. When the snow blows in, enjoy cross-country skiing and sledding in designated areas of the park.

No visit to Ridley Creek Park is complete without a visit to the Hunting Hill Mansion, which also houses the park office. This English-style mansion, complete with manicured gardens and an intricate stone

facade, was built around a colonial farmhouse dating back to 1789. Don't be surprised if you run into some finely-dressed folk while visiting the office; the mansion also serves as a popular wedding venue. History buffs should also visit the Colonial Pennsylvania Plantation, a living history farm in the park that operates from March to December.

Once you've taken the time to explore the beautiful gardens, our hike begins on the White Trail from the parking lot by the Mansion. The peaceful trails are popular for humans and animals, so expect to share the trail with a wide range of creatures; some common wildlife include deer, foxes, and songbirds. You may even spot a great blue heron stalking the creek for its next meal. From the parking lot, you'll take an unmarked dirt path into the woods which quickly opens out onto the paved bike trail. Throughout your counterclockwise loop of the park, you'll frequently pass over this trail. Before getting started on the White Trail, you'll notice a large pollinator garden full of plants native to Pennsylvania, like milkweed and pawpaw trees.

After heading into the woods, you'll stay on the White Trail throughout the hike. Wide and well-marked, the White Trail makes a big loop of the park. The first part of the hike meanders up and down wooded hillsides with just enough elevation to get your heart pumping. Keep your eyes peeled for downed logs on the side of the trail as this is a perfect place to spot fungi. Along the way, the White Trail emerges from the woods to cross roads and bike trails so always take care! You'll cross over bridges and hike alongside gurgling streams as they trickle along to meet up with the creek. After twists and turns through dense woods of oak, beech, and tulip poplar, the White Trail descends to the creekside lowlands. You'll notice light-trunked, towering sycamores lining the shallow waters. Home to flocks of duck, the creek is also a popular spot for fly fishing. Perfectly placed benches encourage hikers to rest and enjoy the quiet trickling of the creek.

## TURN-BY-TURN DIRECTIONS

1. From the kiosk by the parking lot, follow the unmarked dirt trail.
2. At 0.1 miles at a junction with a paved path, turn right; cross the paved path toward the woods following the signs for the White Trail.
3. At 0.4 miles, reach a T-junction with a parking lot access trail. Turn sharply left to stay on the White Trail.
4. At 0.5 miles, turn right to stay on the White Trail.
5. At 0.7 miles, cross a small bridge; 100 feet further, carefully cross the road.
6. At 1.0 miles, cross the road and pass beside the parking lot, continuing on the White Trail.
7. At 1.3 miles, the White Trail joins with the Blue Trail to become the White/Blue Trail; continue straight.
8. At 1.4 miles, where the Blue Trail splits off, continue straight on the White Trail and then cross the road.
9. At 1.6 miles, at a T-junction, make a sharp left, ignoring an unmarked side trail to the road.
10. At 1.7 miles, cross over the paved bike trail.
11. At 2.1 miles, bear left at an intersection where the Yellow Trail joins the White Trail to become the White/Yellow Trail.
12. At 2.4 miles, where the Yellow Trail splits off, turn right to remain on the White Trail.
13. At 2.9 miles, stay straight on the White Trail and then cross the road.
14. At 3.0 miles, reach a creek bed and a bench; immediately afterward, cross the bridge.
15. At 3.5 miles, turn right at a junction with an unmarked trail. A few yards later, turn right again to stay on the White Trail.
16. At 3.8 miles, cross the road to the pavilion areas.
17. At 4.2 miles, turn left, then reach a junction with the bike path and Shady Flash Drive. Use the tunnel on the bike path to go under the road and then turn left back onto the dirt White Trail.
18. At 4.3 miles, turn to the right.
19. At 4.4 miles, reach the junction from Step 2 to complete the White Loop. Take the paved path and trail back to the parking lot.

## FIND THE TRAILHEAD

From West Chester Pike in Newton Square, turn left at the light onto Providence Road. After 1.4 miles, turn right onto Gradyville Road. After 1.0 miles, enter the park and immediately turn left onto Sandy Flash Drive. After 0.3 miles, turn right onto an unnamed road following the signs for the park office and then immediately turn off onto a loop with parking spaces. The trail begins at the kiosk at the far end of the loop.

# LEVANTE BREWING

Levante Brewing may be nestled in a warehouse in West Chester, but the outdoor patio is far from industrial. In fact, founders Tim Floros and Eric Santostefano drew inspiration for their brewery from rustic spots in Italy, where the community gathers around the local drinking hole to sip and socialize. At Levante, whose name comes from "to rise" in Italian, visitors are immediately greeted by a patio full of shade and cozy spots to relax. Plus, there's plentiful seating inside the taproom, and an immediate sense of kinship.

Tim and Eric started off brewing while in college and eventually grew from apartment-sized brew kits to a one-barrel system in Eric's garage. After delighting family and friends with their homebrews, the two realized they might have a hoppy future. It took four years of perfecting their craft and developing a business plan all while juggling day jobs. Finally in 2015, they opened the doors of Levante to the West Chester community and haven't looked back.

Cloudy and Cumbersome is the flagship New England IPA, which they've been brewing up since 2016. It has a balanced hazy profile that pairs perfectly with summers on the patio. The refreshing brew got gold at the Frankfurt international beer trophy in 2022.

## LAND MANAGER

Ridley Creek State Park
Pennsylvania Department of Conservation & Natural Resources
1023 Sycamore Mills Road
Media, PA 19063
(610) 892-3900
www.dcnr.pa.gov/StateParks/FindAPark/RidleyCreekStatePark
Map: elibrary.dcnr.pa.gov/GetDocument?docId=1753216&DocName=RICR_ParkMap.pdf

## BREWERY/RESTAURANT

**Levante Brewing Company**
208 Carter Drive Suite 2
West Chester, PA 19382
(484) 202-0622
www.levantebrewing.com

Distance from trailhead: 11 miles

# VALLEY FORGE

## HIKE THROUGH HISTORY AT A REVOLUTIONARY WAR SITE

| STARTING POINT | DESTINATION |
|---|---|
| YELLOW SPRINGS TRAIL PARKING LOT | MOUNT MISERY |
| **BREWERY** | **HIKE TYPE** |
| ROOT DOWN BREWING CO. | EASY |
| **DOG-FRIENDLY** | **SEASON** |
| YES (LEASH REQUIRED) | YEAR-ROUND |
| **FEES** | **DURATION** |
| NONE | 1 HOUR 30 MIN. |
| **MAP REFERENCE** | **LENGTH** |
| POSTED AT TRAILHEAD | 4 MILES (LOOP) |
| **HIGHLIGHTS** | **ELEVATION GAIN** |
| COVERED BRIDGE, COLONIAL BUILDINGS, HISTORIC BOTTLING FACTORY | 730 FEET |

**7.1%**
**ALCOHOL CONTENT**

## BINE IPA

CLEAR YELLOW

HOPPY

BITTER

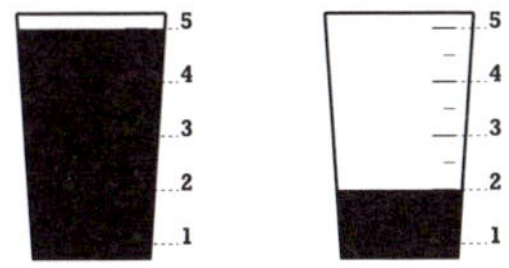

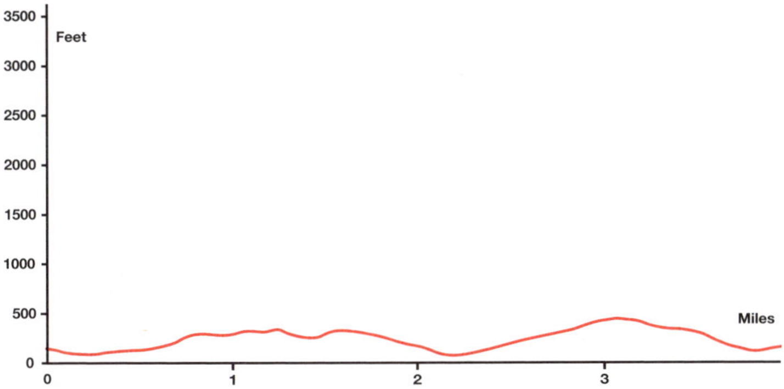

# HIKE DESCRIPTION

**Hike through the colonial encampment that saw Washington's Revolutionary Army through a brutal winter from 1777 to 78. After, head to Root Down Brewing for a brew and a bite in an old root beer factory.**

The winter of 1777 to 1778 at Valley Forge was a brutal time for the ragtag Continental Army. They had weathered many defeats by the British Army and then had to face an unforgiving winter with limited supplies. Although many soldiers perished at Valley Forge, it was also a turning point in the Revolutionary War. During the winter, drill master Baron von Steuben whipped the troops into shape, and France agreed to an alliance with the fledgling nation. Many consider this winter as the birthplace of the American Army. Originally a state park (and Pennsylvania's first state park at that!), today Valley Forge is preserved by the National Park Service, and many of the historic farms and structures are still standing.

Before heading out on your hike, a visit to the museum in the visitor center is a must. The exhibits are a great way to learn more about the Revolutionary War and Valley Forge's significance in the eventual victory for the Continental Army. You can also pick up a map here, which highlights the colonial structures you'll see around the park.

This 4-mile loop hike is a great way to experience some highlights from spots of historical significance to natural beauty. The hike begins a short drive away from the visitor center at the Yellow Springs Parking Lot. You'll start the hike on a wide, sunny path lined by wildflower fields that draw bees and songbirds. The path then passes through a cluster of enormous sycamore trees to cross over Valley Creek. You'll then continue along a wide gravel path past colonial buildings that once housed the officers of the continental army. From there, you'll head into the woods onto lightly trod paths. In the mid-summer, you'll find much of the path lined by wild raspberry bushes. Breaks in the trees make for beautiful overlooks into the surrounding valley. You'll follow the shaded path to the ruins of an old factory that bottled spring water in the early 1900s. The old spring still flows through the ruins of the building.

## TURN-BY-TURN DIRECTIONS

1. From the parking lot, bear left on the road toward Library Lane.
2. At 0.2 miles, turn right onto the Knox Trail, a flagstone path marked by a signpost. After 200 feet, cross the bridge over Valley Creek.
3. At 0.3 miles, reach an interpretive sign for the Officers' quarters. After reading it, continue straight on the trail.
4. At 0.4 miles, turn right to stay on the Knox Trail.
5. At 0.5 miles, turn left to cross the road. In 30 feet, turn left to take the unmarked path through the field.
6. At 0.7 miles, reach a T-junction with a signpost at the top of the hill and then turn left onto the blue-marked Mount Joy Trail.
7. At 1.6 miles, turn left at the fork in the trail to stay on the Mount Joy Trail.
8. At 2.0 miles, turn left.
9. At 2.1 miles, reach Valley Creek Road; keep left and cross the road.
10. At 2.2 miles, turn left onto the Horse Shoe Trail marked by green blazes.
11. At 2.4 miles at the sign post, turn right onto the blue-blazed Colonial Springs Trail.
12. At 2.6 miles, use the bridge to cross the stream. After 50 feet, turn right to stay on the Colonial Springs Trail.
13. At 2.7 miles, pass an abandoned factory on the left.
14. At 3.0 miles, turn left at the Y-junction onto the yellow-blazed Mount Misery Trail.
15. At 3.3 miles, turn right to stay on the Mount Misery Trail.
16. At 3.8 miles, cross Yellow Springs Road and then turn right onto the Yellow Spring Trail. Follow this back to the parking lot.

# FIND THE TRAILHEAD

From the Pennsylvania Turnpike in Valley Forge, take Exit 327 for North Gulch Road. This road becomes Valley Forge Park Road/PA-23 as it leads into the park. Follow the road for 5 miles before making a left turn onto Valley Creek Road/ PA-252. After a mile, turn right onto Yellow Springs Road and pass through the covered bridge. The trailhead is to the left at the end of a gravel road.

# ROOT DOWN BREWING COMPANY

At Root Down Brewing Company, experience the blend of historic and hip with 20th century brick walls decked out with graffiti art and kung fu movies. Situated in a huge space in the heart of downtown Phoenixville, Root Down continues the town's beverage legacy in a space that was once an old root beer factory. Owner Mike Hamara has been in the brew business for decades, from homebrewer in the early 2000s to opening and operating a brew supply store until 2015. It took two years of planning, but finally, Hamara opened the doors to Root Down's 13,000 square foot facility in 2017.

Head Brewer Chris O'Keefe traces his beer past to picking up home brew supplies from Hamara's store. The two formed a friendship which turned into a partnership when Hamara brought him on as assistant brewer. Now at the helm, O'Keefe gets creative with the ever-changing tap rotations and his creations have earned several awards at the Great American Beer Festival.

While jamming to 90s hip hop, enjoy a pour of the award-winning Bine, an easy drinking West Coast IPA that packs a hoppy punch and has been on the tap list since the brewery's early days. There are many drinking options in Phoenixville, but Root Down shines as one of the best. Featuring video games, a full kitchen, and ever changing draft list, this is a must-stop in Eastern Pennsylvania.

## LAND MANAGER

**National Park Service**
1400 North Outer Line Drive
King of Prussia, PA 19406
(610) 783-1000
www.nps.gov/vafo/index.htm
Map: www.nps.gov/vafo/planyourvisit/upload/VAFO-Trail-Map_Mar-2023-Update-v2_16x9.pdf

## BREWERY/RESTAURANT

**Root Down Brewing Company**
1 North Main Street
Phoenixville, PA 19460
(484) 302-5407
www.rootdownbrewing.com

Distance from trailhead: 6.6 miles

# WISSAHICKON VALLEY PARK

### ESCAPE THE CITY GRIND IN THIS URBAN OASIS

| STARTING POINT | DESTINATION |
|---|---|
| VALLEY GREEN ROAD | WISSAHICKON CREEK GORGE |
| BREWERY | HIKE TYPE |
| TWO LOCALS BREWING CO. | MODERATE |
| DOG-FRIENDLY | SEASON |
| YES (LEASH REQUIRED) | YEAR ROUND |
| FEES | DURATION |
| NONE | 2 HOURS |
| MAP REFERENCE | LENGTH |
| ALLTRAILS | 5.1 MILES |
| HIGHLIGHTS | ELEVATION GAIN |
| CREEKSIDE PATH, COVERED BRIDGE, STATUES | 673 FEET |

5.7 %
ALCOHOL CONTENT

## NUBIAN BROWN ALE

DARK COPPER

TOASTED NUTS

MALTY CARAMEL

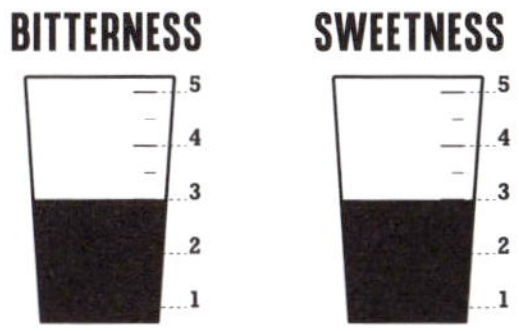


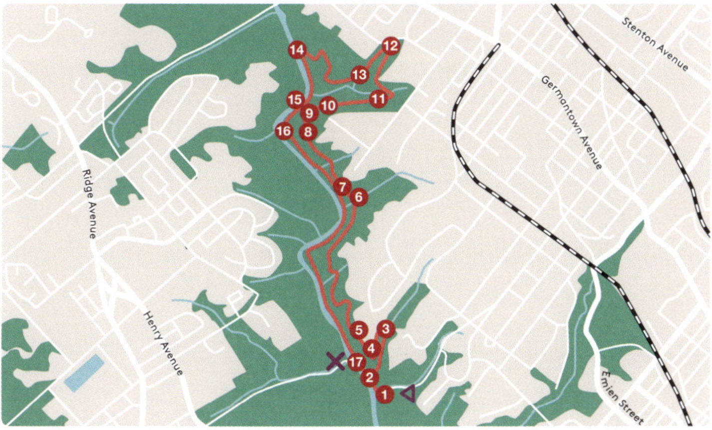


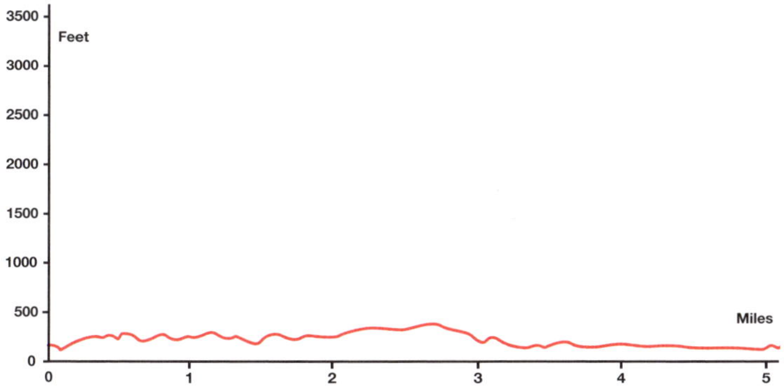

# HIKE DESCRIPTION

**Minutes away from downtown Philly lies the urban oasis of Wissahickon Valley Park. Full of natural and historic landmarks, the wooded trails feel miles away from the bustle of downtown. Afterward, head into town to Two Locals Brewing Company for a hip take on brews and snacks.**

Wissahickon Valley Park is a 1,800-acre urban park that's popular for hiking, biking, and relaxing by the creek. The long narrow park follows along the Wissahickon Creek and the steep gorge it carves into the landscape. Over 50 miles of trails meander through the lush woods, so it's a good idea to have a trail map handy. It's easy to reach the park by public transportation or car; however, like many urban areas, it's best not to leave any valuables in your car. This park is a popular destination, so try to get there early, especially during the summer.

This loop explores the northern section of the park, stopping by just a handful of the many highlights this park has to offer. You'll start off at the Valley Green Road parking lot and initially follow the White Trail, a gravel path that hugs alongside the road. After veering into the woods, you'll come across a small sheltered overlook that gazes out onto the waters of the creek. During the summer, the woods echo with the sounds of laughter as families enjoy creekside picnics. As you peer into the depths of the gorge below and contemplate dipping your toes in the cool water at the end of your hike, keep in mind that swimming in the Wissahickon is prohibited by the City of Philadelphia. After enjoying the views, you'll set course on the White Trail, which travels along the high ground of the gorge.

Meandering through these woods, it's easy to see why poets and artists have long celebrated the dramatic beauty of the Wissahickon Gorge. Even Edgar Allen Poe penned an essay ruminating on the "rare loveliness" of the creek. About a mile and half along, you'll see a large white statue to your left down the hillside. This is a statue of Tedyuscung, once a great leader of the Lenni Lenape people whose homelands included modern day Philadelphia, and is meant to memorialize the displaced people. However, the commanding statue misses the mark by inaccurately portraying a Lenape man, giving him the feathered headdress of the Indigenous peoples of the Great Plains. In spite of the inaccuracies, the statue is a spot to take a moment to acknowledge the Lenape people from whose language the name Wissahickon is derived, meaning yellow-colored stream in the native tongue.

After continuing along the high ground of the White Trail for about a half-mile, you'll get on the Lavender Trail. This path is markedly quieter and more peaceful than the other parts of the park. Towering oak and tulip poplar trees crowd the canopy, reminding you that sections of the park remain an old-growth forest. Take your time wandering through this section as it's an excellent area for birdwatching. In fact,

the park is an Audubon Important Bird Area, providing sanctuary for songbirds, birds of prey, and waterfowl.

At the end of the Lavender Trail, you'll get on the Orange Trail, which travels along the creekside to complete the loop of the park. The path is much more rocky than the higher ground trails. Along the way, notice the red covered bridge, which is the last remaining one of its type in Philadelphia and originally dates back to 1737. This scenic bridge connects the Orange Trail to Forbidden Drive, a former road that now functions as a wide, rocky trail and traverses the length of the park. It's called Forbidden Drive because of a protest in the 1920s when over 13,000 park goers rallied against allowing cars to drive through the park. This successful protest is celebrated yearly with a horseback parade through the park. The last stretch of the trek is particularly rugged, which makes for a fun challenge at the tail-end of your excursion. Along the trail you may enjoy small trickles of water tumbling down the hillside beside you in ephemeral waterfalls after recent rainfall.

## TURN-BY-TURN DIRECTIONS

1. At the trailhead on Valley Green Road, go down the stairs and cross the bridge, then bear to the left on the White Trail.
2. At 0.1 miles, encounter a viewing platform with views of the creek. In a few feet, turn right to take the trail uphill.
3. At 0.3 miles, turn left at the junction.
4. At 0.4 miles, turn left to complete the short loop.
5. At 0.7 miles, stay straight at the trail intersection.
6. At 1.4 miles, continue straight on the white trail.
7. At 1.6 miles, to the left is the statue of Teedyuscung.
8. At 2.0 miles, follow the second left at the junction, then turn right onto the gravel path.
9. At 2.1 miles, turn to the left to get on the Lavender Trail.
10. At 2.3 miles, stay straight at the junction .
11. At 2.7 miles, at the gate, make a sharp left to stay on the Lavender Trail.
12. At 2.8 miles, turn right.
13. At 3.3 miles, turn left to get on the Orange Trail along the creek.
14. At 3.5 miles, encounter a break in the trail, bear to the right.
15. At 3.7 miles, the trail passes the covered bridge. Stay on Orange Trail.
16. At 5.0 miles, turn right to get back onto the White Trail. Retrace your steps back to the trailhead.

# FIND THE TRAILHEAD

From downtown Philadelphia, take I-76 to Route 1. Take the exit for Wissahickon Ave and follow until the end of the road. Make a right on Allan Lane then a left on McCallum Road. Continue through the neighborhood, taking a quick left onto Wolcott Drive, which leads to Valley Green Drive. After entering the park, the parking area is on the right. The trailhead is about 300 feet down the road and begins at the wooden stairs.

## TWO LOCALS BREWING COMPANY

Tucked into a gleaming storefront near Drexel's campus in Philadelphia is Two Locals Brewing Company. Founded by brothers Richard and Mengistu Koiler, this brewery has found a fitting home in the City of Brotherly Love. Richard and Mengistu, the eponymous " two locals," were both raised in West Philly, not far from where their brewery now stands. Richard was working in accounting and Mengistu in finance when they first tried a homebrew kit together. They were immediately hooked and started brewing together on the weekends in Mengistu's backyard.

Rich and Mengistu love craft but often didn't see Black brewers like themselves in the industry. This pushed them to pursue brewing professionally, and in 2018 they officially launched their business. The brothers found a welcoming community in the Philly beer scene where they collaborated with established breweries and often were featured as guest taps while searching for a permanent home of their own. The pandemic was a big set-back, but the brothers never slowed down, even managing to score a distribution contract for home Eagles games. Upon opening in 2024, Two Locals Brewing Company officially became the first Black-owned brewery in Pennsylvania. The taproom features a kitchen menu from local hoagie favorite Liberty Kitchen. It's a collaborative menu, featuring Liberty's classic deli-fresh hoagies, as well as some traditional dishes celebrating the Koiler brother's Liberian and Jamaican heritage. The brothers hope that their brewery will be a welcoming space to diversify the beer industry in Philadelphia and beyond.

Nubian Brown Ale was the first canned beer available from Two Locals, a few years before the opening of the brewery. It pours a richly brown color and its nutty taste pairs perfectly with a steaming bowl of peanut braised eggplant from the kitchen menu.

### LAND MANAGER

**Philadelphia Parks & Recreation**
1515 Arch Street, 10th floor
Philadelphia, PA 19102
+1(215) 683-3600
parksandrecreation@phila.gov
www.phila.gov/departments/philadelphia-parks-recreation

### BREWERY/RESTAURANT

**Two Local Brewing Company**
3675 Market St Suite 100
Philadelphia, PA 19104
(267) 969-3837
www.twolocalsbrewing.com

Distance from trailhead: 10 miles

# NORTHERN NEW JERSEY

# HIGH POINT STATE PARK

## VIEW THREE STATES FROM THE HIGHEST POINT IN NEW JERSEY

MONTAGUE, NJ

**STARTING POINT**
LAKE MARCIA

**BREWERY**
LOG TAVERN BREWING

**DOG-FRIENDLY**
YES (LEASH REQUIRED)

**FEES**
YES

**MAP REFERENCE**
ALLTRAILS

**HIGHLIGHTS**
360 VIEWS, CEDAR SWAMP, APPALACHIAN TRAIL

**DESTINATION**
HIGH POINT MONUMENT

**HIKE TYPE**
MODERATE

**SEASON**
YEAR-ROUND

**DURATION**
1 HOUR 30 MIN.

**LENGTH**
3.7 MILES (LOOP)

**ELEVATION GAIN**
580 FEET

6.3 %
ALCOHOL CONTENT

## LOGTOBERFEST MÄRZEN

DEEP GOLD

MALT-FORWARD

NUTTY

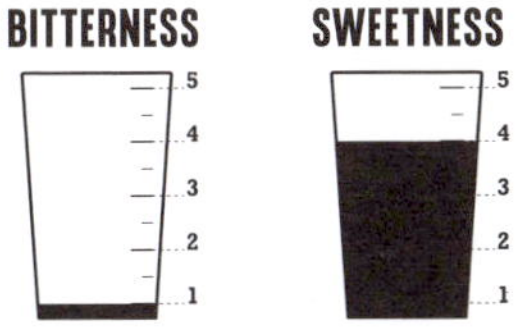


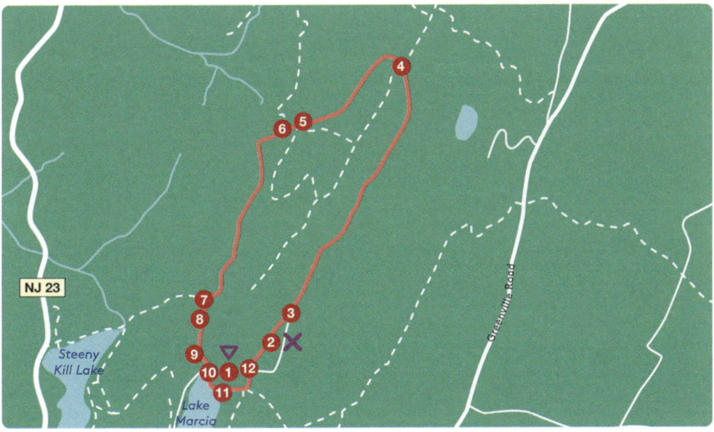


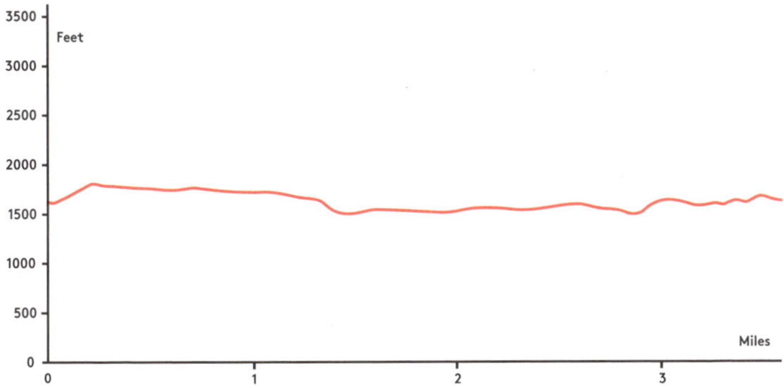

# HIKE DESCRIPTION

**Take this short loop to the highest point in New Jersey with panoramic views of three states. Afterward, visit Log Tavern Brewing for a pint in their rustic taproom just across the PA border.**

High Point State Park is a haven in Northern New Jersey for hikers and outdoor enthusiasts. With mountainous terrain and upland swamps, this region known as Skylands is markedly different from the rest of the state, which is more flat and coastal. With its proximity to large metro regions, the park is a popular weekend destination for those looking to get out on its over 50 miles of trails.

There are several spots throughout the park to access the Monument Loop, but this route begins at the parking lot beside Lake Marcia, where swimming is allowed in the summer months. Other lakes in the park also allow kayaking, fishing, and boating. Within the first

quarter-mile of the hike, you'll reach the white obelisk emerging from the trees like a beacon for hikers and park-goers; this is High Point Monument, which was built nearly one hundred years ago to honor war veterans. At just over 1,800 feet, the summit with High Point Monument has the honor of being the highest point in New Jersey. From here, you'll enjoy stunning panoramic views of the Pennsylvanian Poconos Mountains to the west, the Catskills of New York to the north, and the New Jersey Wallkill River Valley to the south. These views are especially beautiful at sunset.

From the monument, the oak-lined trail follows along the ridge before heading down to skirt around the Dryden Kuser Natural Area where you'll find an Atlantic white cedar bog. These coastal trees are a keystone species to the ecosystem, providing essential water filtration from pollutants and providing habitats for endangered species like the Swamp Pink, a native wildflower, and the Timber Rattlesnake. You usually won't find Atlantic white cedars at elevations over 150 feet, however, thanks to the acidic peat soil and standing water, here they stand at nearly 1,800 feet. Past the swamp, the terrain becomes rocky again before letting out along the shore of Lake Marcia. Before completing the monument loop, you'll pass a junction with the Appalachian Trail, which runs for eighteen miles in the park.

## TURN-BY-TURN DIRECTIONS

1. From the parking lot at Lake Marcia, head straight up on the Monument Trail to the right of the restrooms, marked by a red/green blaze on metal signs on trees.
2. At 0.2 miles, reach High Point Monument and the viewing platform to the left. After taking in the views, continue on the Monument Trail.
3. At 0.5 miles, pass through the parking lot to continue on the Monument Trail at the far end of the lot.
4. At 1.6 miles, cross over the blue-marked trail to stay on the red/green-marked Monument Trail.
5. At 2.1 miles, continue straight at the fork to stay on the Monument Trail.
6. At 2.2 miles, turn left to stay on the Monument Trail.
7. At 3.0 miles, at a T-junction, go slightly left and up the hill.
8. At 3.1 miles, go up the stone stairs.
9. At 3.2 miles, the trail meets the paved road. Turn left toward the lake.
10. At 3.3 miles, passing by the parking lot from step 1, the trail begins again along the lake shore.
11. At 3.4 miles, at a Y-junction, turn left away from the lake and then cross a road. In 200 feet, reach a 4-way junction with the Appalachian Trail turn left to stay on the Monument Trail.
12. At 3.5 miles, reach a junction and turn left to return to the parking lot.

## FIND THE TRAILHEAD

From NJ-23 in Wantage, proceed for 4.6 miles. At the High Point Cross Country Ski Center, turn right onto the park road. After 1.0 miles, find the parking lot with bathrooms on the left side of the road. Lake Marcia will be to the right of the road. The Monument Trail starts to the right of the restroom building. Alternatively, you can park at the Monument, but the lot fills very quickly.

# LOG TAVERN BREWING

Mildford, Pennsylvania was the home of Gifford Pinchot, the founder and first head of the US Forest Service and one of the instigators of the modern American conservation movement. It seems fitting then that this is the same town where you can find Log Tavern Brewing, a company with a love of the great outdoors at its heart. Thanks to co-owners Ryan Scott and Joe Fischer's tireless redesign work, you'd never believe that this cozy taproom was once a lackluster industrial building. The taproom is modeled after a rustic cabin, and don't be surprised if you spot Big Foot; hey, he likes beer too! After snapping a photo with the sasquatch photo cutout, head to the bar to check out the impressive mix of beer styles on tap. A crisp pour of Logtoberfest pairs perfectly with a cool evening on the brewery's back patio, complete with fire pits. The caramel malty flavor will have you dreaming of escaping to a log cabin of your own.

## LAND MANAGER

**New Jersey State Park Service**
1480 State Route 23
Wantage, NJ 07461
(973) 875-4800
nj.gov/dep/parksandforests/parks/highpointstatepark.html
Map: www.nj.gov/dep/parksandforests/parks/maps/HighPointTrails FinalDraft_reduced.pdf

## BREWERY/RESTAURANT

**Log Tavern Brewing**
309 East Harford St, Building 2
Milford, PA 18337
(570) 212-9642
www.logtavernbrewing.com

Distance from trailhead: 14 miles

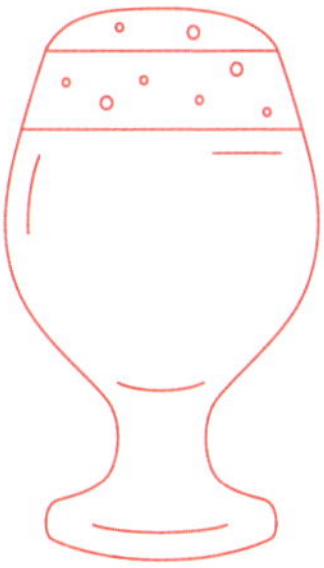

# STAIRWAY TO HEAVEN

## MARSHES TO MOUNTAINS ON THE APPALACHIAN TRAIL

| STARTING POINT | DESTINATION |
| --- | --- |
| STAIRWAY TO HEAVEN PARKING | PINWHEEL VISTA |
| **BREWERY** | **HIKE TYPE** |
| ALIAS BREW WORKS | STRENUOUS |
| **DOG-FRIENDLY** | **SEASON** |
| YES (LEASH REQUIRED) | YEAR-ROUND |
| **FEES** | **DURATION** |
| NONE | 3 HOURS |
| **MAP REFERENCE** | **LENGTH** |
| ALL TRAILS | 6.8 MILES (OUT AND BACK) |
| **HIGHLIGHTS** | **ELEVATION GAIN** |
| STONE STEPS, VIEWS, BOARDWALK | 1,105 FEET |

**4.5%**
ALCOHOL CONTENT

## SEASON OF THE STONE SAISON

GOLDEN

FRUITY

BUBBLY, APRICOTS

BITTERNESS

SWEETNESS

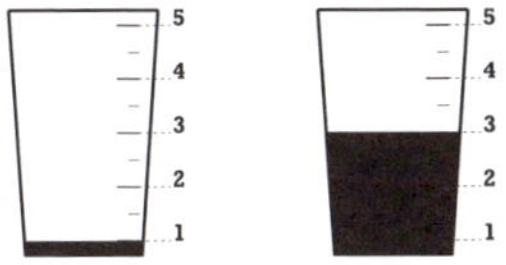


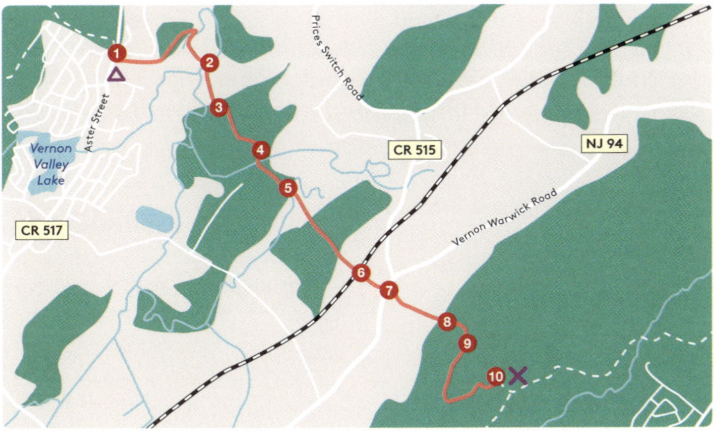


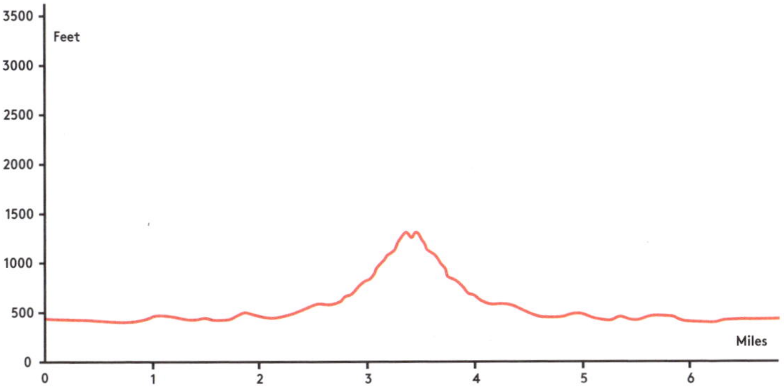

# HIKE DESCRIPTION

**Hike along boardwalks over wetlands to a rocky hill climb, ending with a dramatic vista. Afterward, visit Alias Brewing, the brewery super group of Two Villians Brewing and Muckraker Beermaker for a wide selection of sours, lagers, and more.**

The Appalachian Trail traverses 72 miles across Northern New Jersey, passing through rugged hills and over boggy wetlands. This out-and-back section of the trail near the New York border offers some of the best New Jersey landscape on the AT. Throughout its 4,000-mile journey, the Appalachian Trail is always marked by white blazes.

The journey begins at the Appalachian Trail access point on McAfee Greenwood. You'll immediately start on the wooden boardwalk, called the Pochuck Boardwalk. Appalachian Trail volunteers built this mile of raised path completely by hand. Tall grasses surround the boardwalk that red-winged blackbirds flit in and out of. About halfway along the boardwalk, you'll cross the 110-foot Pochuck Suspension bridge, also constructed by volunteers; this impressive bridge took three years to complete.

Once you reach the end of the boardwalk, you'll head into the woods on a narrow dirt path. You might be sharing the way with other day hikers and also thru-hikers (people hiking the entire length of the AT). About a mile and a half in, you'll briefly join up with a bike path before continuing on the AT. No vehicles, including bikes, are allowed on the long-distance trail. From here, the trail alternates between wooded dirt trails and plank walkways through tall grasses. At around 2 miles, you'll carefully cross railroad tracks and climb the wooden stile over the chain link fence. You'll emerge into a wide cow pasture, but please heed the sign and do not approach any livestock. Ahead, Wawayanda

Mountain Ridge rises in the distance. After crossing through the field and resisting the urge to make bovine friends, carefully cross over Vernon Warwick Road. This is an alternate parking area if you only wish to do the Stairway part of the hike. The trail picks up again at the rear of the parking area.

You'll continue straight along the flat trail through open fields dotted with trees. Up until now, you've had a pretty flat hike. But that all changes once you head into the tree line. Suddenly, the landscape changes, and large boulders rear up from the ground. At about 2.5 miles, you'll start up the rock "stairway." The rugged way is steep, with stone slabs strategically placed to create steps. After nearly a mile (and 1,000 feet of elevation) later, you'll crest the ridge and see a large rock pile. Follow the blue blazes from the pile to take a spur trail to the overlook. Look for the wooden sign for Pinwheel Vista. This is a wide rocky expanse with stunning views of the surrounding farmland. Looking closely, you can see the cow pasture you walked through just a few miles ago! You can even see the High Point State Park monument rising in the distance on very clear days. Once you've had your fill of the spectacular view, turn around and retrace your steps exactly back to the beginning of the boardwalk.

## TURN-BY-TURN DIRECTIONS

1. From the parking area along the side of the road, start on the Appalachian Trail boardwalk beside the trailhead kiosk.
2. At 0.7 miles, cross the creek using the suspension bridge.
3. At 0.9 miles, leave the boardwalk and head into the woods, continuing on the white-blazed Appalachian Trail.
4. At 1.3 miles, turn right onto a bike trail. Proceed for 200 feet, then turn left to leave the bike trail and continue along the Appalachian Trail.
5. At 1.5 miles, use the bridge to cross the stream.
6. At 2.1 miles, cross the railroad tracks, then climb the short ladder over the fence. Head into the cow pasture but do not approach the cattle.
7. At 2.2 miles, carefully cross the road. The trail begins again at the far side of the parking ahead. Take the wooden steps to continue.
8. At 2.6 miles, the trail leaves the open meadow and heads into the woods. Continue straight.
9. At 2.7 miles, pass between two large rocks and then continue up the rocky "stairs."
10. At 3.4 miles, turn left at the large rock pile and follow the sign for Pinwheel Vista. The view begins 100 feet ahead. Retrace steps back along the same path to return to the parking area.

## FIND THE TRAILHEAD

From Hamburg, head north on NJ-94. Continue for 2.6 miles, then stay straight at the traffic light to get onto McAfee Glenwood Road. Proceed for 3.8 miles, then turn left at the stop sign onto North 517. Continue for 1.7 miles, then park on the side of the road for the trailhead. Be mindful of the "no parking" signs and do not park in the neighborhood where it is permit-parking only. The trail begins to the right of the parking area by the large trail kiosk.

# ALIAS BREW WORKS

Two Villians Brewery joined forces with Muckraker Beermaker in 2024 to create the Alias brand. The tongue-in-cheek collaboration allows the two breweries to be completely expressive in their own brands while coming up with new brews under one umbrella. At Alias, there's something for every palate, from distinctive wild ales and easy-drinking lagers, to hop-forward IPAs.

Tom Troncone, owner and brewer at Muckraker Beermaker, left a fast-paced career as a newspaper reporter in the Big Apple to focus on his homebrewing. With Muckraker being a colloquial term for an investigative journalist, Tom's brewery name combines his career paths: Muckraker Beermaker. He opened in rural Sussex County, New Jersey, the northernmost brewery in the state in 2019. Tom specializes in wild beers and loves to experiment with spontaneous fermentation.

Jonathan Fernandez and Sean Stampfl have been friends for over 20 years and have brewed together for almost as long. They often bumped into Tom Troncone at homebrew competition and the three quickly became friends. After four years of learning the ropes of commercial brewing, Jonathan and Sean decided to strike out on their own. In 2019, they opened Two Villians Brewing in Nyack, New York. The two enjoyed several years of serving on Main Street before making the difficult decision to close the taproom. All was not lost for the two villains though. In 2023, they joined forces with Tom to open Alias Brew Works. The new location is tucked into the resort area of Northern New Jersey where hiking and outdoor opportunities abound.

Season of the Stone is a summer saison refermented on apricots and bottle-conditioned to perfection. The crisp, almost champagne-like bubbles are perfect for porch sipping and toasting to another season of warm nights and outdoor adventures.

## LAND MANAGER

**Appalachian Trail Conservancy**
799 Washington Street,
PO Box 807
Harpers Ferry, WV 25425
(304) 535-6331
https://appalachiantrail.org/
Map: www.appalachiantrail.org/explore/hike-the-a-t/interactive-map

Distance from trailhead: 6 miles

## BREWERY/RESTAURANT

**Alias Brew Works**
17 Old Rudetown Road
Vernon Township, NJ 07462
www.aliasbrewworks.com

# BUTTERMILK FALLS AND CRATER LAKE LOOP

## WATERFALLS, LAKES, AND PONDS, OH MY!

WALPACK TOWNSHIP, NJ

| STARTING POINT | DESTINATION |
| --- | --- |
| BUTTERMILK FALLS PARKING LOT | CRATER LAKE |
| **BREWERY** | **HIKE TYPE** |
| ANGRY ERIK BREWING | STRENUOUS |
| **DOG-FRIENDLY** | **SEASON** |
| YES | SPRING TO FALL |
| **FEES** | **DURATION** |
| NONE | 3 HOURS |
| **MAP REFERENCE** | **LENGTH** |
| POSTED AT TRAILHEAD | 6.1 MILES |
| **HIGHLIGHTS** | **ELEVATION GAIN** |
| TWO LAKES, WATERFALL, APPALACHIAN TRAIL | 1,381 FEET |

6.1%
ALCOHOL CONTENT

LEAF ERIKSON HARVEST ALE

PUMPKIN ORANGE

CRISP

NUTTY CARAMEL

BITTERNESS

SWEETNESS

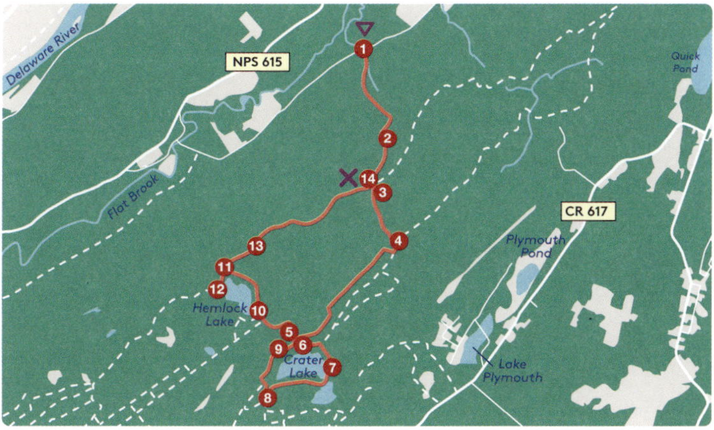


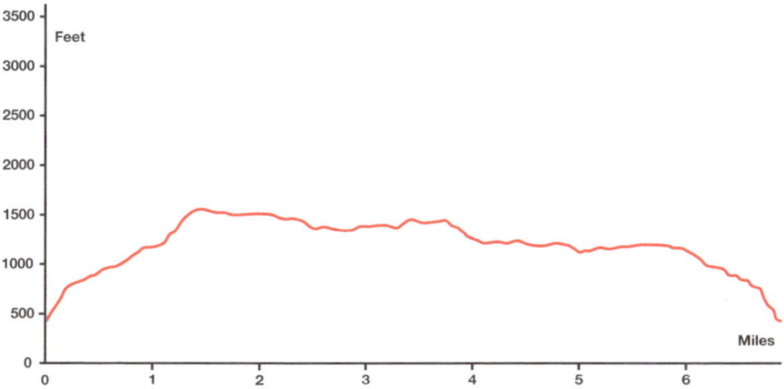

# HIKE DESCRIPTION

**Hike up the side of Buttermilk Falls, the highest waterfall in New Jersey, and past two lakes for a challenging but rewarding 6-mile loop. Afterward, rest your feet at Angry Erik Brewing and have a brew at the Viking ship-themed bar.**

In a region known for its waterfalls, you don't have to go far on this hike to enjoy New Jersey's tallest falls: it's right at the trailhead! Buttermilk Falls is located in the Delaware Water Gap National Recreation Area. This land is managed by the National Park Service and spans nearly 40 miles of the Delaware River across New Jersey and Pennsylvania.

On the left-hand side of the falls you'll take a series of stairs that go up and up. Take advantage of several viewing platforms along the way to admire the falls and catch your breath. At the top of the stairs, you'll have another 1,000 feet to climb on rocky paths for around a mile and a half. Finally, the trail meets up the Appalachian Trail (AT) where it becomes flatter and easier to traverse.

Around 2 miles into the hike, you'll encounter Crater Lake, a glacial lake formed nearly 20,000 years ago when receding glacial carved out a depression in the earth and filled it with meltwater. Being in a rather remote area of the Water Gap Region, this lake is very peaceful and a good spot to stop for a break. The lake is also accessible by a seasonal road and has pit toilets by the picnic area on the east side of the lake.

After looping around the lake, you'll return to the AT and follow signs for Hemlock Pond. From here, the trail plunges into dark hemlock woods with the needles softening most sounds. Around 0.4 miles through the woods, you'll reach a pristine pound with crystal clear water reflecting the surrounding hemlock trees. Tucked far away from any roads, this pond is a beautiful reward for anyone willing to make the trek!

From there, it's an easy way back to Buttermilk Falls Trail and down to the parking lot. These remote woods are chock full of flora and fauna, like many varieties of mushrooms and migratory birds. If visiting in May or June, expect to see huge rhododendron bushes exploding in color!

## TURN BY TURN DIRECTIONS

1. The trail begins at the stairs beside the waterfall. There is a kiosk with the map and area information next to the stairs.
2. At 0.7 miles, pass a small waterfall on the left of the trail.
3. 1.0 miles, cross over the Woods Trail and follow the blue markings on trees and rocks.
4. At 1.4 miles, turn right onto the white-marked Appalachian Trail (AT) and then immediately make another right to stay on the AT.
5. At 2.3 miles, turn left to stay on the AT.

6. At 2.4 miles, turn left, heading off the AT and onto the marked Crater Lake loop.
7. At 2.7 miles, pass a pier looking out onto the lake.
8. At 3.2 miles, turn right, returning to the white-marked AT.
9. At 3.7 miles, turn left to stay on the AT and then continue straight onto the Hemlock Pond Trail marked with green and orange paint on trees.
10. At 4.1 miles, turn right onto the Blue Mountain Lake Trail marked with green paint on trees.
11. At 4.4 miles, turn left to the Hemlock Pond viewpoint. Once at the viewpoint, turn around and retrace your steps back to the Blue Mountain Lake Trail.
12. At 4.7 miles, continue straight onto Wood Road.
13. At 5.0 miles, pass a small swamp with a stream crossing.
14. At 5.8 miles, turn left on the Buttermilk Falls Trail to return to the parking lot.

## FIND THE TRAILHEAD

From Blairstown, NJ take Milbrook Road north for 7 miles. Turn right onto Old Mine Road and follow it for 2.2 miles. At the Old Flat Brook Bridge, turn right onto Walpack Flatbrook road (NPS Service Road 615) and proceed for 3.2 miles. Bear to the right on Haney's Mill Road and then right again after 0.4 miles onto Mountain Road. The parking lot will be on the right 1.4 miles down the road beside the Buttermilk Falls sign. The trailhead is on the left side of the street beside the waterfall.

## ANGRY ERIK BREWING

Angry Erik Brewing is the joint venture of Heide and Erik Hassing who left big league careers to follow their passion of craft beer. Years ago, in between pursuing degrees and climbing the career ladder in NYC, the couple found a love for homebrewing. Pretty soon, the homebrewing outgrew their NYC apartment and they moved to the Jersey suburbs where they experimented further with brewing larger and larger batches. Eventually the couple took the leap in 2014 to open a small taproom on the weekends.

Erik's past as a criminal prosecutor in NYC gave the brewery's name, as he was known as "Angry Erik" in the courtroom. Meanwhile, as head brewer, Heide's past life studying biochemistry and culinary arts has allowed her to craft some truly unique beers. The couple regularly switches up the taps and tries new beers so patrons can enjoy new flavors with each visit as well as a few long-standing favorites. Leaf Erikson Harvest Ale is a satisfying nod to the fall season with a comforting taste of baking spices reminiscent of a homemade pie. It's perfect for shorter days and cool evenings.

The most striking part of Angry Erik? The bar is modeled after a to-scale Viking ship. The mast soars behind the taps and the ship's dragon figurehead looms as a scaly referee for cornhole games on the patio.

## LAND MANAGER

**Delaware Water Gap National Recreation Area**
P.O. Box 2
Bushkill, PA 18324
(570) 426-2452
www.nps.gov/dewa
Map: www.nps.gov/dewa/planyourvisit/maps.htm

## BREWERY/RESTAURANT

**Angry Erik Brewing**
2 Camre Dr,
Newton, NJ 07860
(862) 432-9003
www.angryerik.com

Distance from trailhead: 16 miles

# MOUNT TAMMANY

## GORGEOUS VIEWS OF THE DELAWARE WATER GAP

| STARTING POINT | DESTINATION |
|---|---|
| DUNNFIELD CREEK NATURAL AREA | MOUNT TAMMANY |
| BREWERY | HIKE TYPE |
| BUCK HILL RESTAURANT & BREWERY | STRENUOUS |
| DOG-FRIENDLY | SEASON |
| YES (LEASH REQUIRED) | YEAR-ROUND |
| FEES | DURATION |
| NONE | 2 HOURS 30 MIN. |
| MAP REFERENCE | LENGTH |
| ALLTRAILS | 3.7 MILES (LOOP) |
| HIGHLIGHTS | ELEVATION GAIN |
| VIEWS, APPALACHIAN TRAIL, WATERFALL | 1,250 FEET |

**5.3%**
**ALCOHOL CONTENT**

## CLIFFS RED ALE

AMBER

LIGHTLY HOPPY

CRISP,
TOFFEE

BITTERNESS

SWEETNESS

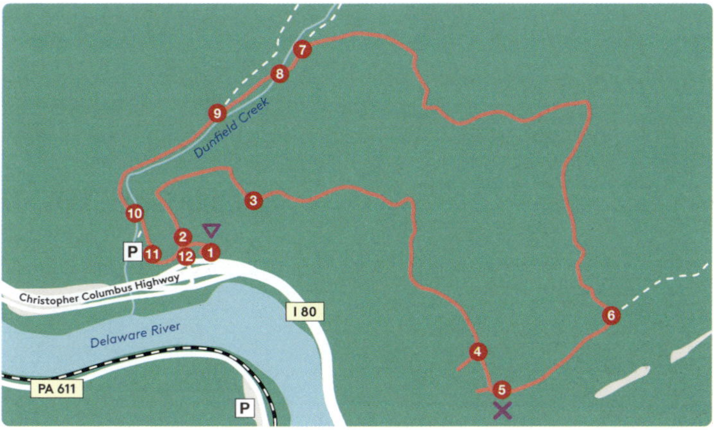


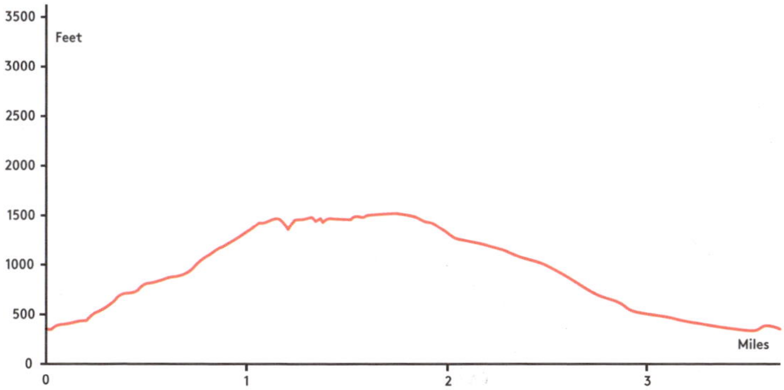

# HIKE DESCRIPTION

**Climb rocky hills for a dramatic view of the Delaware Water Gap and end with a pleasant creek hike with waterfalls. Afterward, refuel at the farm-to-table Buck Hill Brewery and Restaurant.**

With stunning overlooks of the Appalachian Mountains, it's easy to see why Mount Tammany is one of New Jersey's most popular hikes. The loop is not for the faint of heart though, gaining over 1,000 feet of elevation in the first mile. Following the Red Dot and Blue Trails will lead you through both Worthington State Forest and the Delaware Water Gap National Recreation Area.

You can access the trail by either of the two parking areas off I-80, but be aware that they fill up quickly on weekends. Throughout the hike, keep an eye out for red circles on a white background on trees and rocks to guide your way. You'll immediately start uphill on wooden steps, at the top of which, transitions into a dirt path lined by trees. Within the first quarter mile, you'll also climb large rock stairs and

scramble over exposed bedrock. After around a half mile, you'll get the first look at the rushing Delaware Water Gap below on the right. A water gap is a place where a stream or river has carved a pass through a mountain ridge or range. In this area, the Delaware River cuts through the Appalachian Mountains, not only forming the gap but also acting as a natural border between Pennsylvania and New Jersey. The dramatic region formed through hundreds of millions of years of water and glacial ice erosion. Mount Tammany itself was named for Tamanend, the Lenni-Lenape chieftain who signed peace treaties with William Penn in the 17th century.

After clambering over rocky steps and large boulders, you'll get a reprieve by taking a side trail to the first of the main overlooks. Although this is not the highest point, it's a lovely wide rock ledge that provides a stunning view of Mount Minsi, the sister mountain of Mount Tammany. The second of the main overlooks is only a few hundred feet up the trail and is the closest the trail gets to the 1,526-foot summit of Mount Tammany. Getting to the second overlook requires a difficult rocky downhill scramble, but the challenge of getting to the overlook makes the view all the more beautiful! Be sure to rest and watch the birds of prey like vultures and hawks swooping through the air below you.

After soaking in the views, you'll get on the Blue Trail to begin the descent. This trail takes a wide path around the far side of the peak. It's far less steep than the way up, although still quite rocky. You'll follow this gentle route through peaceful hemlock groves before meeting the picturesque Dunnfield Creek lined with spring-blooming rhododendrons and mountain laurels. There are several spots where you can go to the water and see small waterfalls cascade over the rocks. As the warning signs state, swimming is not allowed, but it's a perfect spot to rest and bask in the beauty of the Dunnfield Natural Area. There is a bench overlooking the small Dunnfield cascades and the larger falls are about 200 feet down the trail. You'll then follow the trail, now marked by blue and green blazes, as it meanders along the creekside and finish your trek on the white-blazed Appalachian Trail.

## TURN-BY-TURN DIRECTIONS

1. From the parking lot, take the Red Dot Trail to the right of the picnic tables, marked by a brown sign and red blaze.
2. At 0.1 miles, turn right to stay on the Red Dot Trail, marked by red dots on a white back on trees and rocks.
3. At 0.4 miles, reach a vista of the mountains across the water gap.
4. At 1.1 miles, take the unmarked side trail to the right for access to a scenic viewpoint on a wide flat rock.
5. At 1.3 miles, follow the white arrows down a rocky scramble to the main vista. After, turn around and climb back up the rocks. At this point, the trail becomes the Blue Trail marked by blue blazes. Continue along the Blue Trail.
6. At 1.7 miles, reach a Y-junction; turn left to stay on the Blue Trail, ignoring the fire road to the right. Proceed along the Blue Trail.
7. At 2.9 miles, the Blue Trail meets up with the Dunnfield Creek Trail; turn left to continue on the joint Blue and Dunnfield Creek Trail (Green).
8. At 3.0 miles, use the bridge to cross the creek.
9. At 3.1 miles, the trail meets up with the white-blazed Appalachian Trail; turn left to follow the Appalachian Trail alongside the creek.
10. At 3.4 miles, cross another bridge over the creek and follow the trail to one of the parking lots.
11. At 3.5 miles, after looping around the parking lot, get back on the Red Dot Trail, marked by a brown sign on the left side of the lot.
12. At 3.6 miles, reach the same junction from Step 2. Turn right, and in 0.1 miles return to the parking lot to complete the hike.

## FIND THE TRAILHEAD

From Warrington, New Jersey, get on I-80 West. Proceed for 3 miles; then take the right exit lane to follow the brown sign for Dunnfield Creek/Appalachian Trail. The exit lane splits in two; remain in the far right lane which immediately leads to the first parking lot. If this lot is full, turn right out of the parking lot back to the road. Proceed for 500 feet and the secondary parking lot will be on the right. Be aware that you cannot backtrack to the first lot without getting back onto I-80 West.

# BUCK HILL RESTAURANT AND BREWERY

After years of watching a prime restaurant property sit vacant, Jay Mena took matters into his own hands. He purchased the building and in 2016 opened Buck Hill Restaurant. Jay and master brewer Bud Usinowicz wanted to create a destination brew pub that would draw people to the small town of Blairstown. When they got the brewery up and running in 2017, it became the first brewpub in Warren County.

At Buck Hill, it's a true farm-to-table experience. Most of the menu items, from hardy pub grub, like burgers, to more elevated fish and pasta entrees, are sourced from farms in northern NJ. Jay calls their brewery "farm to foam" since most of the finishing hops are grown locally at the Buck Hill Farm. The cycle continues with the spent grain from the brewing process going back to the local farms to feed livestock.

Throughout the process of opening Buck Hill, Mena used all local builders and designers to create a truly bespoke space. A hand-hewn wooden front door and custom iron railing by local artisans are two features that help create the rustic yet regal ambiance. The inside is spacious with separate bar and dining room areas, and there is a multi-level outdoor space to sip your brews al fresco. A pint of the Cliffs Red Ale tastes delightful while lounging next to the outdoor fireplace. Named for Assistant Brewer Nick's red husky, Clifford, this amber-hued brew is the perfect balance of hops and malty sweetness.

## LAND MANAGER

**New Jersey State Park Service**
Worthington State Forest
2 Old Mine Road
Columbia, NJ 07832
(908) 841-9575
www.nj.gov/dep/parksandforests/parks/worthingtonstateforest.html
Map: nj.gov/dep/parksandforests/maps/worthington-area.pdf

## BREWERY/RESTAURANT

**Buck Hill Brewery & Restaurant**
45 NJ-94
Blairstown, NJ 07825
(908) 854-5300
www.buckhillbrewery.com

Distance from trailhead: 13 miles

# SCHOOLEY'S MOUNTAIN PARK

## WATERFALLS ABOUND IN THIS SUBURBAN TREASURE

| STARTING POINT | DESTINATION |
| --- | --- |
| FAIRVIEW AVE PARKING LOT | ELECTRIC BROOK WATERFALLS |
| BREWERY | HIKE TYPE |
| CHILTON MILL BREWING | MODERATE |
| DOG-FRIENDLY | SEASON |
| YES (LEASH REQUIRED) | YEAR-ROUND |
| FEES | DURATION |
| NONE | 1 HOUR 30 MIN. |
| MAP REFERENCE | LENGTH |
| ALLTRAILS | 2.4 MILES (LOOP) |
| HIGHLIGHTS | ELEVATION GAIN |
| LAKE, BOULDERS | 600 FEET |

**6.0 %**
ALCOHOL CONTENT

**SCHWARZBIER BLACK LAGER**

BLACK

SMOKY

SMOOTH, MALTY

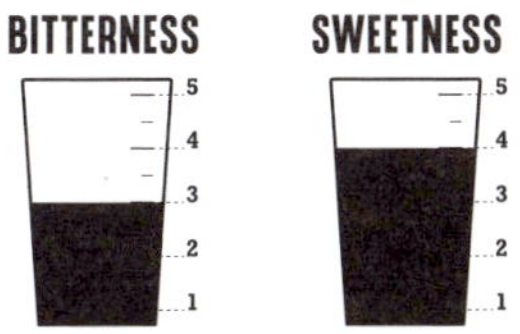


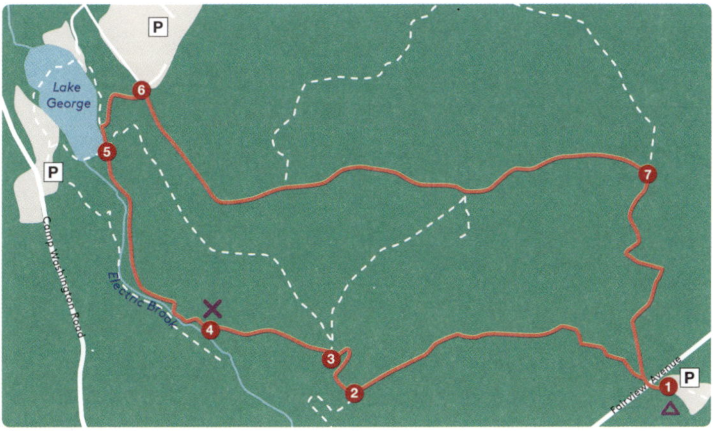


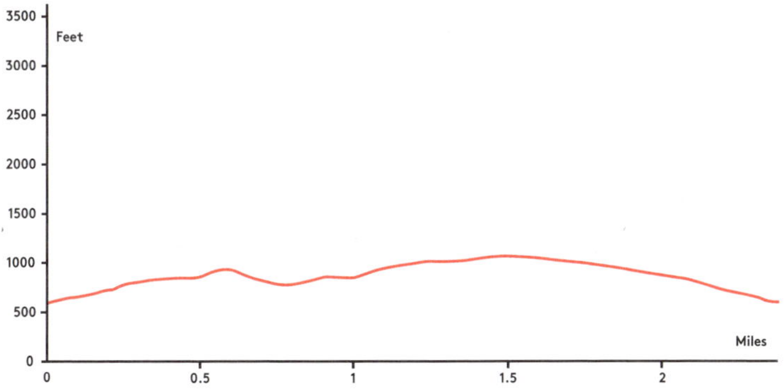

# HIKE DESCRIPTION

**Take this short but rocky hike along a brook as it cascades through a boulder-lined valley. Afterward, head to nearby Chilton Mill Brewing for unique takes on classic beer styles in a cozy taproom.**

Spanning 823 acres in the rolling hills of Washington Township, Schooley's Mountain Park is a delight for hikers of all ages. Your hike begins at the large gravel parking lot on Fairview Avenue, where you'll cross the quiet street and set out on the Patriot's Path, marked by a sign with white paint and a small map kiosk. The rocky trail heads uphill, passing through groves of young hardwood trees frequently covered in lichen. Within the first mile, the uphill path opens onto a large rocky outcropping, which offers an overlook of the surrounding farmlands and gently rolling hills in the distance.

The outcropping also serves as a trail junction, so be sure to keep an eye on the colored markings on the trees. After the overlook, you'll get on the Blue Trail heading down into the stream valley. The trail becomes significantly more rocky and makes for a fun and challenging descent toward the stream. This stream is known as Electric Brook because its waters were used to power a hydroelectric plant in the 1920s. Ahead, you'll see the main waterfall as it tumbles over boulders. To the left, several short, unmarked trails will lead you down to the waterside for the best views of the cascades.

After enjoying the view of the waterfall from below, take the stone steps that hug the side of the boulder to climb to the top of the waterfall. From here, you'll follow the brook as the water spills over small rocks. A bench sits alongside the water, which makes for a perfect photo.

Hiking uphill, you'll head toward another waterfall. This one is manmade and at its base you can see the ruins of the old electric plant that used this dam to generate electricity. After a brief, steep incline, you'll leave the tree cover and emerge onto Lake George. Created by damming the small brook, Lake George is a lovely spot to stop and take in the scenery. On the opposite side of the lake is the Lodge pavilion, which often hosts small wedding ceremonies at the lakeside chapel. You'll walk along the lake until you bear right and reach another parking area with bathrooms, pavilions, and sports fields. From here, you'll follow the Yellow Trail into the deciduous forest and remain on this peaceful path back to the trailhead.

## TURN-BY-TURN DIRECTIONS

1. From the parking lot, cross the road and find the trailhead marked by a small kiosk and a wooden sign for the Patriot's Path. Head into the woods and in a few feet, turn left on to the Patriot's Path, marked by white blazes and metal discs on trees.
2. At 0.5 miles, turn right at the Y-junction to stay on the Patriot's Path.
3. At 0.6 miles, encounter a rocky outcropping to the left that overlooks the valley. 20 feet down the path, there is a convergence of several trails; turn left to take the Blue Trail, ignoring the teal/ white and pink trails.
4. At 0.8 miles, reach the waterfall. To the left is a small, unmarked spur trail that leads closer to the water for a better view of the falls. Once you've enjoyed the falls, return to the Blue Trail and continue along Electric Brook.
5. At 1.1 miles, reach Lake George and follow the Blue-Blazed Trail as it hugs the right bank of the lake. After 100 feet, turn right onto the unmarked gravel path leading uphill into the trees.
6. At 1.2 miles, the gravel path lets out onto Park Road, where you'll find bathroom facilities and a large parking lot straight ahead. Make a sharp right, away from the parking lot to return to the white-blazed Patriot's Path as it heads into the woods. In 100 feet, the Patriot's Path splits off to the right; ignore this and keep left to stay on the now Yellow-Blazed Trail.
7. At 2.0 miles, turn right at the Y-junction to continue on the Yellow-Blazed Trail as it switchbacks down the hillside before ending at the trailhead.

## FIND THE TRAILHEAD

From Hackettstown, head southeast on Main Street. Continue for 0.5 miles at which point Main Street turns slightly left and becomes US-46 East/Mill Street. After 1.2 miles, turn right onto Reservoir Road. After 2 miles, turn right onto Naughright Road and proceed for 2.8 miles. At a four-way intersection, turn right onto Fairview Avenue. After 1.2 miles, the trail parking lot will be on the left with a wooden sign for Langdon Palmer Fishing Access Area.

# CHILTON MILL BREWING

Chilton Mill Brewing is tucked into a snug storefront in Long Valley, New Jersey. What the brewery lacks in space, it makes up for in community and delicious beer. Owner and brewer Mike Peachey had a similar start to a lot of brewery owners: he started out homebrewing and began to share with his friends. When they started wanting to buy bottles, Mike knew that he had something worth pursuing.

After years of perfecting recipes, Mike and his wife Laura opened their doors in 2019 and quickly became a local favorite for their commitment to traditional beer styles. Despite the small operation, Mike typically has eight taps flowing, featuring standard IPAs, funky sour creations, and traditional brews like pilsners and tripels. Their Schwarzbier, winner of a silver medal at an international beer competition, is a delicious lager that's incredibly smooth and explodes with a roasty aroma. Mike is very proud of this beer; while it takes upwards of 8 weeks to brew, it's frequently on tap because it's so sought-after by the local community!

## LAND MANAGER

**Morris County Parks Commission**
300 Mendham Road
Morris Township, New Jersey 07960
(973) 326-7631
www.morrisparks.net
Map: www.morrisparks.net/wp-content/uploads/2023/04/TrailMap_SM.pdf

## BREWERY/RESTAURANT

**Chilton Mill Brewing**
59 East Mill Road
Long Valley, New Jersey 07853
www.chiltonmillbrewing.com

Distance from trailhead: 1.5 miles

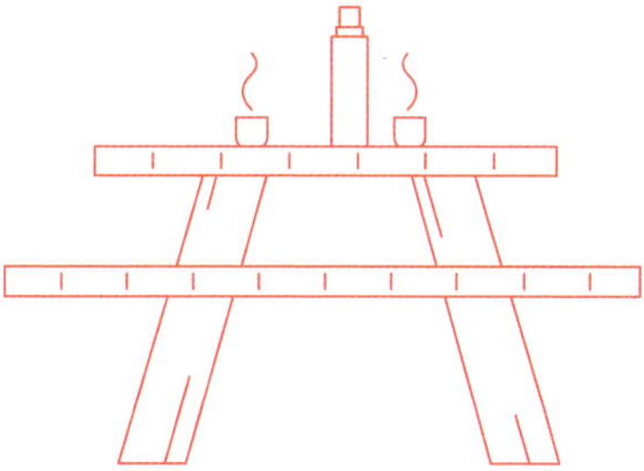

# SOUTH MOUNTAIN RESERVATION

## A DELIGHTFUL SCULPTURE GARDEN AND WATERFALL

| STARTING POINT | DESTINATION |
| --- | --- |
| SHADY NOOK PICNIC AREA | HEMLOCK FALLS |
| **BREWERY** | **HIKE TYPE** |
| TWIN ELEPHANT BREWING CO. | EASY |
| **DOG-FRIENDLY** | **SEASON** |
| YES (LEASH REQUIRED) | YEAR-ROUND |
| **FEES** | **DURATION** |
| NONE | 2 HOURS |
| **MAP REFERENCE** | **LENGTH** |
| SOUTH MOUNTAIN CONSERVANCY TRAIL MAP | 5.1 MILES (LOOP) |
| **HIGHLIGHTS** | **ELEVATION GAIN** |
| WATERFALL, SCULPTURES | 518 FEET |

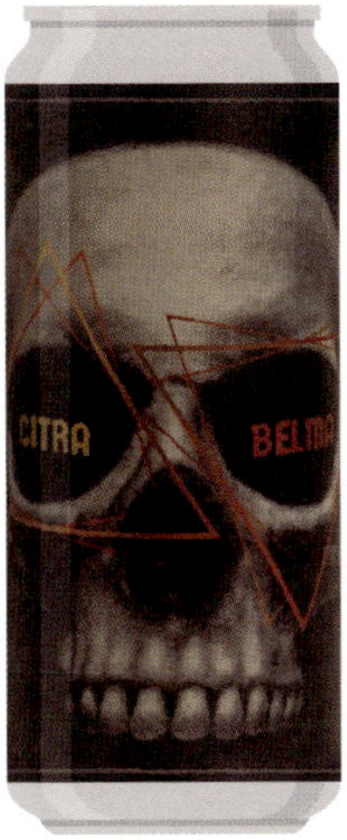


**7.0 %**
ALCOHOL CONTENT

## CITRA & BELMA IPA

OPAQUE YELLOW

TROPICAL

SWEET,
RICH

BITTERNESS

SWEETNESS

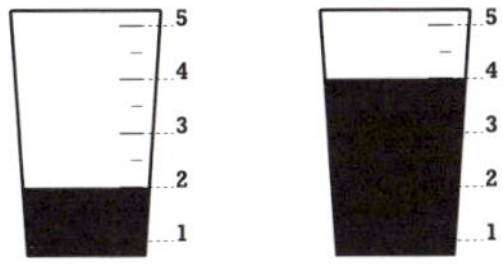

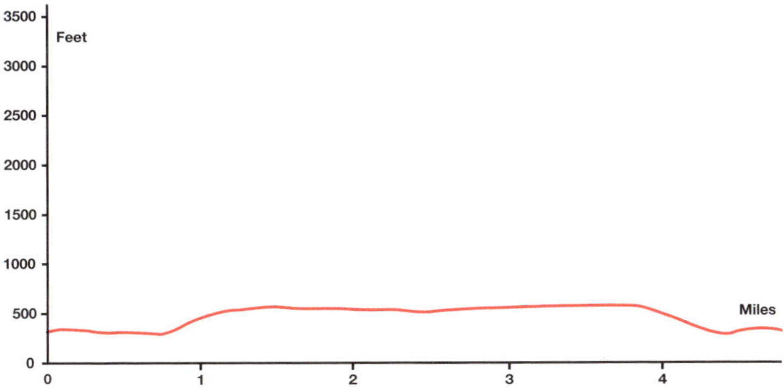

# HIKE DESCRIPTION

**Explore this county park in the New Jersey suburbs to see a 25-foot waterfall and a public sculpture garden. After your ramble in the woods, cheer your efforts with a brew at Twin Elephant Brewing at their inviting outdoor patio and plant-filled taproom.**

Amidst the suburbs of Essex County lies the 2,000-acre South Mountain Reservation. This wooded park is full of meandering trails that tempt you to put the map away and just get lost. Surrounded by densely-populated counties and only about 20 miles away from downtown New York, this wooded park is a surprising green oasis. South Mountain Reservation is a popular destination, so expect to share the trails with other day hikers. However, the more than 15 miles of trails offer plenty of opportunities to escape the crowds.

The main highlight of the park is the centrally-located and accessible 25-foot Hemlock Falls, which you'll come across about a half mile into the hike. The beginning of this hike is on the Lenape Trail, a 36-mile trail that links 18 different parks in the county! At the north end of South Mountain Reservation is the Turtle Back Zoo, which is a great spot for families. Around three and a half miles in, you'll pass the Wildflower Sculpture Park, a rotating public art exhibit featuring contemporary artists. Often the pieces incorporate the natural landscape.

Back in Revolutionary War times, a patriot beacon was placed on the high point of the park (now called Washington's Lookout) to observe British troops in New York. After years of industry in the area, the local government created the Essex County Parks Commission to reclaim and preserve the land. In the 1930s, the Olmsted Brothers (landscape architecture legends) designed the park while the Civilian Conservation Corps carried out much of the construction. Now, it remains a key part of the Essex County park system.

Despite the name, you won't be climbing any mountains in this park. However, gently rolling hills and a varied landscape make for an enjoyable hike. During the springtime, keep an eye out for wildflowers and blooming rhododendrons. As many of the trails intersect, there are many opportunities to shorten or lengthen this 5-mile loop. Be sure to purchase a map from the Conservancy or follow along Alltrails to avoid getting too turned about on these intricate trails.

## TURN-BY-TURN DIRECTIONS

1. From the Shady Nook Picnic site, cross the street to get on the yellow-blazed Lenape Trail.
2. At 0.1 miles, at the four-way junction, bear right, staying on the Lenape Trail.
3. At 0.4 miles, at an junction, turn left on the Lenape Trail following the signpost toward Hemlock Falls.
4. At 0.6 miles, encounter the falls. Once you've had your fill, turn around and retrace your steps back along the Lenape Trail to the intersection in the previous step; from here, turn left.
5. At 0.9 miles, go up the stone steps and then turn right.
6. At 1.1 miles, turn right at the fork. In 150 feet, turn right again onto the red-marked Summit Trail.
7. At 2.6 miles, at a T-junction, bear left on a gravel path; immediately after, turn left onto the Crest Drive Trail.
8. At 3.5 miles, turn left on an unmarked trail. In 150 feet, turn right onto the wide path looping around the Summit Field picnic area.
9. At 3.8 miles, cross the road and pass a parking lot; the trail continues behind the parking lot.
10. At 4.0 miles, turn left onto the Lenape Trail and follow it back to the parking lot.

## FIND THE TRAILHEAD

From I-78 near Millburn, take Exit 49A to merge onto NJ-124W. At the end of the ramp, turn right at the light onto Main Street. After 1.1 miles, make a slight right at the traffic light onto Brookside Drive, which leads into the park. After 2.5 miles, turn right onto Cherry Lane. The picnic area parking will be ahead on the left at the end of the road. The trailhead starts at the yellow trail marker beside the kiosk.

# TWIN ELEPHANT BREWING COMPANY

In 2016, three homebrewing friends, Cynthia Derama, Tim Besecker, and Scott McLuskey finally took the leap to start a brewery and created Twin Elephant. McLuskey, an identical twin himself, says the brewery's name refers to the rarity of twins in elephant species. This is fitting as the brewery has become a popular spot in Morris County for unique, small-batch brews. Like many New Jersey breweries, there's no kitchen, but patrons are encouraged to bring food or order takeout from a local restaurant. Most of the taproom, including the outdoor space, is lovingly crafted from reclaimed wood, lending a rustic yet chic look. Twin Elephant specializes in IPAs and the Citra and Belma is one of their Nosh series, which takes drinkers on a hoppy adventure. This iteration features Citra and Belma hops which combine for a juicy IPA that's thirst-quenching on a hot day.

## LAND MANAGER

**Essex County Department of Parks, Recreation, and Cultural Affairs**
155 Prospect Avenue, Suite #100
West Orange, NJ 07052
(973) 268-3500
www.essexcountyparks.org/parks/south-mountain-reservation/partners#48
Map: essexcountyparks.org/parks/south-mountain-reservation

## BREWERY/RESTAURANT

**Twin Elephant Brewing Company**
13 Watchung Avenue
Chatham, NJ 07928
(973) 507-9862
www.twinelephant.com

Distance from trailhead: 7 miles

# DEVIL'S HALF-ACRE

## ROCKY SCRAMBLES ABOUND

| STARTING POINT | DESTINATION |
| --- | --- |
| SOURLAND MOUNTAIN PRESERVE PARKING | DEVIL'S HALF-ACRE BOULDERS |
| **BREWERY** | **HIKE TYPE** |
| FLOUNDER BREWING CO. | MODERATE |
| **DOG-FRIENDLY** | **SEASON** |
| YES (LEASH REQUIRED) | YEAR ROUND |
| **FEES** | **DURATION** |
| NONE | 2 HOURS 30 MIN. |
| **MAP REFERENCE** | **LENGTH** |
| POSTED AT TRAILHEAD | 5.6 MILES (LOOP) |
| **HIGHLIGHTS** | **ELEVATION GAIN** |
| BOULDERS, POND, WOODLANDS | 600 FEET |

**5.0%**
ALCOHOL CONTENT

## HILL STREET HONEY BLONDE ALE

STRAW

GRAINY

HONEY, FLORAL

BITTERNESS

SWEETNESS

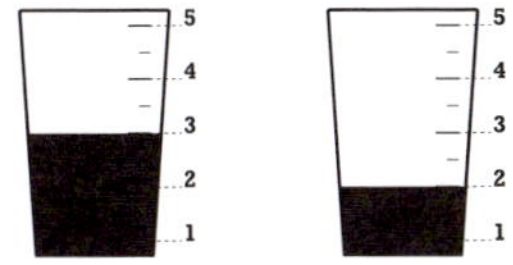


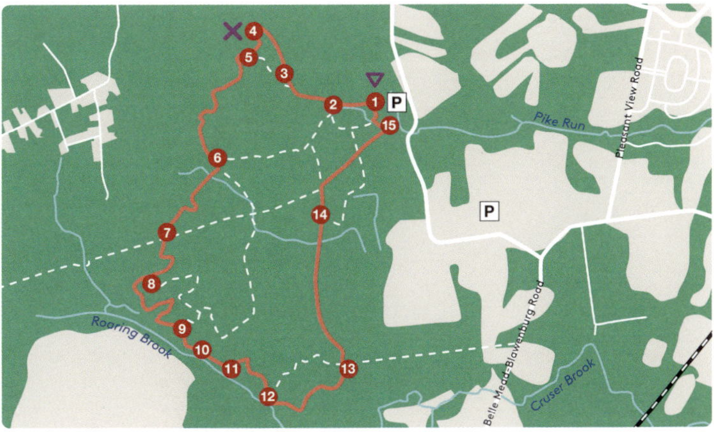


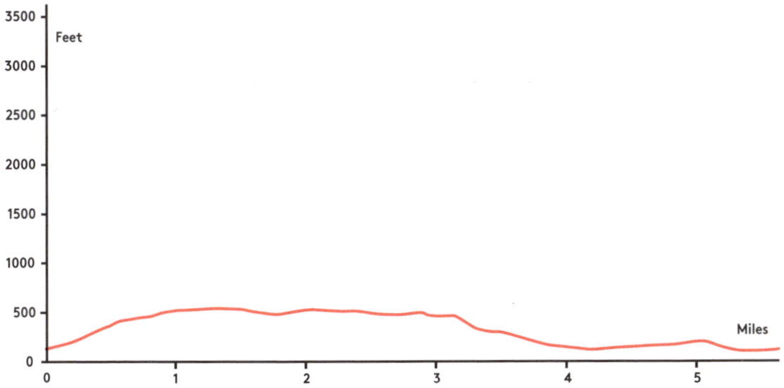

# HIKE DESCRIPTION

**Clamber over massive boulders and through peaceful woods along the Devil's Half-Acre in Central New Jersey. Then, kick back and relax with a pint in the historic barn-turned-taproom at Flounder Brewing Co.**

Despite reaching just shy of 600 feet at its highest point, Sourland Mountain rises steeply from the surrounding farmland. Hence, the locals christened it a mountain. You'll set out at the preserve's large parking lot. The park is extremely popular on the weekends and the Devil's Half-Acre is the most popular trail, so you'll want to aim for a morning or evening outing, outside of peak hiking times. Once on the trail, it's easy to navigate with clear color-coded trails and markers at major intersections to help orient hikers.

You'll begin at the White Trail kiosk with a detailed preserve map. Make sure to take a picture, as the posted map doesn't always align with popular trail apps. Then, get ready to climb, because most of the hike's 600 feet of elevation is all in the first half-mile!

Most of the way is very rocky and uneven, so careful footing is a must. At the end of the incline, your reward is fascinating rock formations; some of the massive boulders are as big as a house! The freeze/thaw cycles of water during the Ice Ages slowly shifted these erosion-resistant igneous boulders from higher up in the mountains. The yellow-marked Devil's Half-Acre Trail winds between the ancient rocks. Light bouldering is welcome, but not necessary to continue along the trail. You'll also pass by a large tree defiantly growing out of a split boulder. Even a tiny sapling can widen fractures in a boulder over decades.

After leaving the main boulder section, you'll notice that the woods become quieter. The tall deciduous trees, including sassafras, maple, beech, oak, and more, create a dense canopy of green overhead. After a mile and a half on the Devil's Half-Acre Trail, you'll start on the red-blazed Ridge Trail. Large rocks embedded in the trail keep the trek interesting. Although the origin is unclear, many think Sourland refers to how the rock-filled terrain made the land "sour" for farming. It may be sour for crops, but sweet for a hike!

At about 2 miles, you'll cross through a grassy field before getting on the blue-marked Roaring Rocks Trail, which passes over another boulder field. Believe it or not, a stream runs 15 feet beneath these boulders. After the boulder field, you'll traverse along boardwalks over rocky patches and creek beds. After an easy walk, you'll emerge onto the wide open Pipeline Trail. This expanse filled with grasses and wildflowers lets out next to a small pond. You'll finish your hike with a loop around the waters, which is home to many frogs and turtles. The benches lining the pond make it the perfect spot to rest after completing your hike.

## TURN-BY-TURN DIRECTIONS

1. From the parking lot, begin at the trailhead with the white kiosk. Follow the gravel path into the woods to start on the Maple Flats Trail, marked by a wooden post with orange trail blazes.
2. At 0.2 miles, keep right at the Y-junction with a post saying "Trail Marker #1" to leave the orange blazes and get on the yellow-blazed Devil's Half-Acre Trail. Do not take the bridge to the left.
3. At 0.5 miles, stay on the Devil's Half-Acre Trail heading to the right.
4. At 0.8 miles, cross over a large boulder section known as the Devil's Half-Acre.
5. At 0.9 miles, pass between two large boulders, then follow the trail as it turns right to leave the boulder area.
6. At 1.7 miles, reach Trail Marker #3. Turn right onto the white-marked trail. In 100 feet, turn right to begin the red-blazed Ridge Trail.
7. At 2.2 miles, cross through an open grassy field before heading back into the woods.
8. At 2.5 miles, at the Y-junction, stay right to remain on the Ridge Trail.
9. At 3.1 miles, reach Trail Marker #4. Turn right to leave the Ridge Trail and begin on the blue-blazed Roaring Rocks Trail to pass through another boulder area.
10. At 3.3 miles, continue straight on the Roaring Rocks Trail.
11. At 3.4 miles, reach Trail Marker #5. Go straight to leave Roaring Rocks Trail and get on the white-blazed Tributary Trail.
12. At 3.8 miles, continue straight on the Tributary Trail.
13. At 4.3 miles, after going over the boardwalks, reach Trail Marker #7. Continue straight on the Tributary Trail.
14. At 4.9 miles, reach Trail Marker #8. At this intersection, leave the Tributary Trail to get back on the orange-blazed Maple Flats Trail. Continue straight for 300 feet, then turn right to get on the Pipeline Trail toward the parking lot.
15. At 5.5 miles, turn left to loop around the small pond before returning to the parking lot.

## FIND THE TRAILHEAD

From Princeton, New Jersey, take Route 206 north for 8 miles. At a traffic light, turn left onto Trent Place. Proceed for 0.8 miles at which point Trent Place becomes Belle Mead-Blawenburg Road. Continue for 0.3 miles, then turn right onto East Mountain Road. After 1.1 miles, the Preserve entrance will be on the left, marked by a green and white sign. Continue on the driveway for 0.1 miles; the parking lot will be straight ahead. The trail begins at the white kiosk to the right.

# FLOUNDER BREWING CO.

It's hard to beat having a delicious beer in an 18th-century barn and that's exactly what you get when you visit Flounder Brewing at Carriage Farms. With indoor and outdoor seating, this breezy venue beckons you to slow down and take a load off. But the brewery wasn't always so sprawling. When homebrewer Jeremy Lees decided to start brewing commercially, it was on a one-barrel system in an industrial park garage. Along with his brother Dan and cousin Billy Jordan, the tiny operation was the smallest brewery in New Jersey when it opened in 2013. They didn't have a taproom and only sold growler pours on select weekends per month. In 2016, the lucky owners won a brewer grant, which allowed them to expand operations and start welcoming patrons to a small taproom. The space quickly became popular, with the Brewer's Association naming Flounder one of the nation's fastest-growing breweries in 2018. At that time, the owners started to look at expanding further and landed on the beautiful farm property. Jeremy, Dan, and Billy finally welcomed patrons to the new space in 2021.

From the very beginning, Hill Street Honey Ale was a staple of Flounder. Jeremy first started brewing it in his Morristown apartment on Hill Street, back when brewing was just a hobby. Today, it's still the most popular beer at the taproom. As a nod to his beekeeping grandfather, the ale is brewed with orange blossom honey. The slightly sweet draft is perfect for enjoying at one of the tap room's picnic tables overlooking the farmland.

## LAND MANAGER

**Somerset County Park Commission**
355 Milltown Road
Bridgewater, NJ 08807
(908) 722-1200
www.somersetcountyparks.org
Map: www.somersetcountyparks.org/sites/g/files/vyhlif8281/f/uploads/sourland_mountain_preserve_map_0.pdf

## BREWERY/RESTAURANT

**Flounder Brewing Co.**
2 Clerico Lane, Building 4,
Hillsborough Township, NJ 08844
www.flounderbrewing.com

Distance from trailhead: 5.5 miles

# SOUTHERN NEW JERSEY

# CHEESEQUAKE STATE PARK

## A MARSHLAND TREK ON THE RARITAN BAY

| STARTING POINT | DESTINATION |
|---|---|
| GORDON ROAD PARKING LOT | HOOKS CREEK |
| **BREWERY** | **HIKE TYPE** |
| ALTERNATE ENDING BEER CO. | MODERATE |
| **DOG-FRIENDLY** | **SEASON** |
| YES (LEASH REQUIRED) | YEAR-ROUND |
| **FEES** | **DURATION** |
| YES | 2 HOURS |
| **MAP REFERENCE** | **LENGTH** |
| NJ STATE PARKS BROCHURE | 4.0 MILES (LOOP) |
| **HIGHLIGHTS** | **ELEVATION GAIN** |
| SALT AND FRESHWATER MARSHES, CEDAR SWAMPS | 266 FEET |

**7.5 %**
ALCOHOL CONTENT

## WHAT IF? IPA

HAZY GOLD

CITRUS

SMOOTH & PINEY

BITTERNESS

SWEETNESS

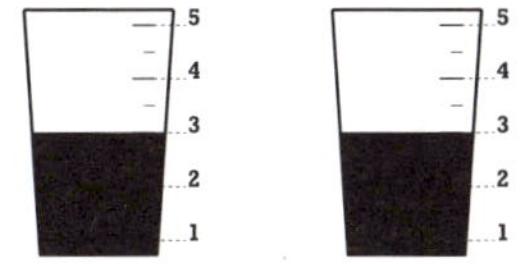


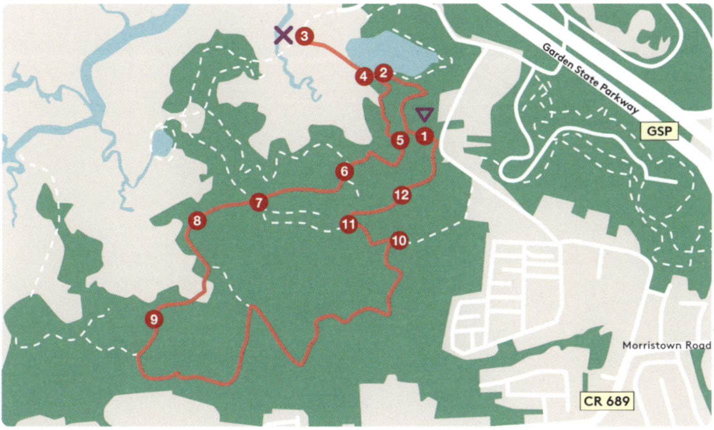


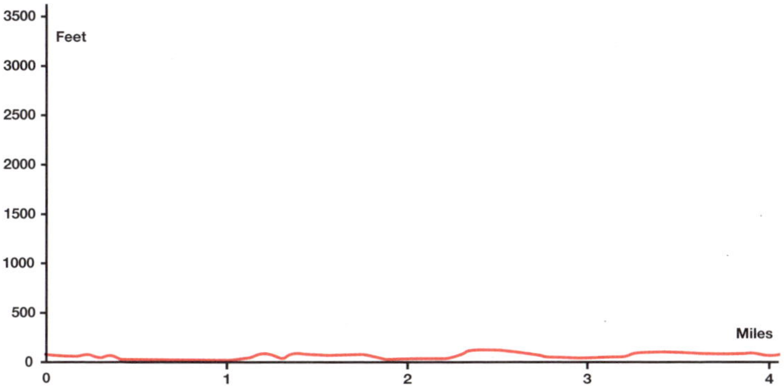

# HIKE DESCRIPTION

**Experience a biodiverse transitional landscape from forests to swamps at Cheesequake State Park. After exploring the trails and boardwalks, head to Alternate Ending Brewing for food and brews in an old movie theater.**

Cheesequake State Park is a 1,610-acre treasure of the New Jersey Park System because of its unique geographical location. The Garden State Parkway bisects the park, nestling it between urban and suburban areas. *Cheseh-oh-ke* means "upland" in the Native American Lenape language, an apt name for a park only a few miles up-land from the Raritan Bay. Cheesequake Park offers an extraordinary meeting of two ecosystems—saltwater marshes and inland deciduous forests.

The journey begins at the parking lot on Gordon Road at the trailhead for four of the main park trails. The park is divided into five main trail systems of different colors—Green, Yellow, Red, Blue, and White. This loop explores the Green and Yellow trails for a modest 4-mile hike that provides a full loop of the diverse ecosystems Cheesequake State Park has to offer. Although you can enjoy this hike any time of the year, its proximity to water can make it buggy in the summer and icy in the winter.

You'll start the hike by following the Yellow Trail on a sandy singletrack path and then down stairs to the marshes. Along the Yellow Trail, you'll pass saltwater marshes full of grasses and reeds and the pungent smell of saltwater. With their high tolerance for salt, eastern red cedars grow tall along the edges of the marsh. In some of the marshes, you'll see the lettuce-like leaves of skunk cabbage, a sign of a freshwater marsh. After around a half mile of hiking along the marshes, you'll pass the 11-acre Hooks Creek Lake and head to the boardwalk where you may see people crabbing off the pier. From here, you'll turn around and follow back along the Yellow Trail for a half mile before turning onto the Green Trail for a wide loop of the inland deciduous forest ecosystem. Along the Green Trail, you'll follow along boardwalks and stairs over sandy soil. About a quarter-mile in, you'll pass the Nature Center where you can stop in to learn more about the ecosystems in the park. After hiking along the wetlands, notice how the landscape changes to silty soil and towering hardwood trees, like maples and oaks. After around 3 miles through the forest, you'll loop back to the parking lot for the end of the hike.

## TURN-BY-TURN DIRECTIONS

1. From the parking lot, start at the wooden arch; in a few feet, turn right onto the Yellow Trail, marked by yellow stickers affixed to posts.
2. At 0.4 miles, descend the stairs and then turn right, following along the lake.
3. At 0.6 miles, reach an intersection; turn right onto the marked Blue Trail to reach a viewing platform on the creek in 100 feet. From here, turn around and retrace your steps along the lake back to the intersection at step 2.
4. At 0.9 miles, turn left on the Yellow Trail; do not take the stairs from step 2.
5. At 1.1 miles, turn left at the intersection to leave the Yellow Trail and get on the marked Green Trail on a boardwalk.
6. At 1.4 miles, after going up a set of stairs, reach a fork and turn left to stay on the Green Trail.
7. At 1.6 miles, cross Petrine Road and continue on the Green Trail.
8. At 1.8 miles, turn left at a T-junction to stay on the Green Trail.
9. At 2.2 miles, cross Museum Road and stay on the Green Trail.
10. At 3.5 miles, turn left at the T-junction onto Campground Road.
11. At 3.7 miles, turn right off the road onto the marked Red and Green Trail, a dirt path looping around the campground.
12. At 3.8 miles, the trail returns to Museum Road; turn right onto Museum Road and follow the road back to the parking lot.

## FIND THE TRAILHEAD

From Matawan, head north on NJ-34. After 1.7 miles, turn right onto Disbrow Road. After 0.4 miles, turn right onto Morristown Road. Continue for 0.4 miles, then turn left onto Gordon Road. After 0.8 miles, the park office will be to the right. After passing the park entrance, the trail parking lot will be on the left with signs for the Nature Center. Begin the hike at the large wooden arch.

## ALTERNATE ENDING BEER CO.

Owner and founder Scott Novick found his own alternate ending in the form of an unexpected corporate layoff which turned into the chance to start a new career as a brewer. After years of gaining experience in the industry, Scott was ready to give an old movie theater in his hometown an alternate ending too.

Now, that movie theater is a family-friendly brewery that pairs top notch beer, a love of movies, and a full menu through a partnership with Talula's Pizzeria. Alternate Ending offers a full grub menu, including Talula's famous sourdough pizza. On the weekends, stop in for a nostalgic 80's-themed brunch inspired by *The Breakfast Club*.

When it comes to beer, Alternate Ending is not afraid to experiment. Expect to see a variety of styles on the menu, from easy drinking lagers to funky sours. A pub favorite is the flagship hazy IPA, What If? This easy-drinking IPA packs all the piney citrus flavor of an IPA with the juicy smoothness of a hazy beer. When the beertender asks if you want another, you won't hesitate to say, "Why Not?"

## LAND MANAGER

**New Jersey State Park Service**
300 Gordon Road
Matawan, NJ 07747
(732) 566-2161
www.nj.gov/dep/parksandforests/parks/cheesequakestatepark
Map: nj.gov/dep/parksandforests/maps/cheesequake-area.pdf

## BREWERY/RESTAURANT

**Alternate Ending Beer Co.**
1057 NJ-34
Aberdeen Township, NJ 07747
(732) 612-8422
www.aebeer.com

Distance from trailhead: 4.3 miles

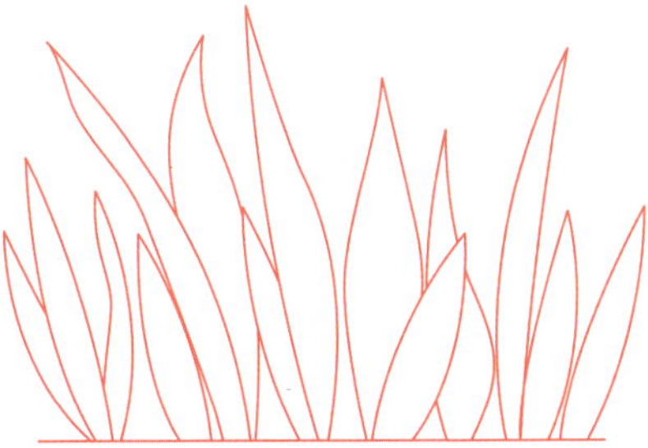

# HARTSHORNE WOODS PARK

## EXPLORE AN OCEAN-VIEW PARK WITH MILITARY HISTORY

| STARTING POINT | DESTINATION |
|---|---|
| ROCKY POINT TRAIL | BATTERY LEWIS |
| BREWERY | HIKE TYPE |
| CARTON BREWING CO. | MODERATE |
| DOG-FRIENDLY | SEASON |
| YES (LEASH REQUIRED) | YEAR-ROUND |
| FEES | DURATION |
| NONE | 1 HOUR 30 MIN. |
| MAP REFERENCE | LENGTH |
| ALLTRAILS | 3.3 MILES (LOOP) |
| HIGHLIGHTS | ELEVATION GAIN |
| HISTORIC BATTERY, OCEAN VIEWS, RIVER PIER | 360 FEET |

**4.0 %**
ALCOHOL CONTENT

## CARTON OF MILK SESSION NITRO MILK STOUT

BLACK

SWEET

SMOOTH, CREAMY

BITTERNESS

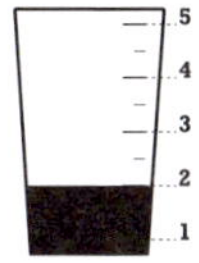


SWEETNESS

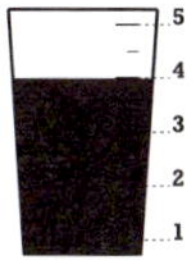


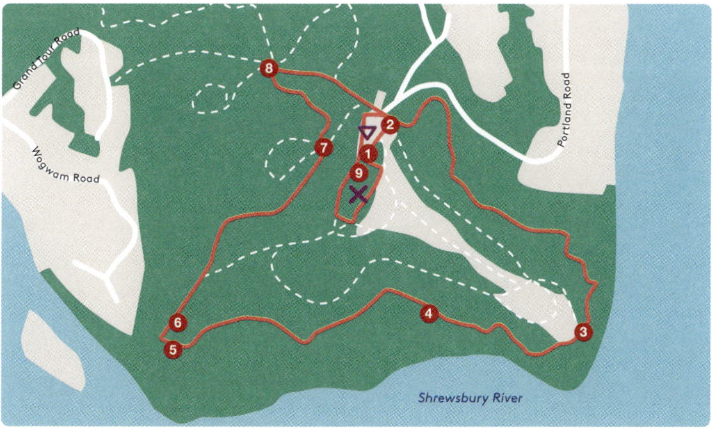


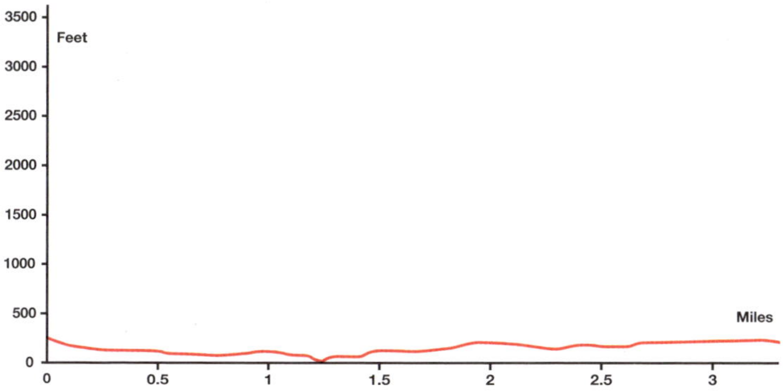

# HIKE DESCRIPTION

**Ramble through remnants of a coastal defense site in this shore-side wooded park. After enjoying the trails, head to Carton Brewing for a milk-inspired pint in the seashore town of Atlantic Highlands.**

This coastal park is located in the Bayshore Region of New Jersey, known for its proximity to Sandy Hook Bay and Sea Bright beaches. A thin strip of barrier islands separate Hartshorne Woods Park from the Atlantic Ocean. The Monmouth County Park System diligently maintains the sixteen miles of paved and natural trails.

Three main areas split up Hartshorne Woods: Buttermilk Valley, Monmouth Hills, and Rocky Point. Although the park is beautiful all year round, some of the vistas are best seen in winter when fewer leaves

obscure the scenery. The hike begins at the Battery parking lot and guides you along the black-blazed Rocky Point Trail on packed sand paths. Within the first half-mile, you'll head into a forest of young tulip poplars, maples, and other hardwood trees with a dense undergrowth of brambles and holly.

Throughout the loop, you'll enjoy several viewpoints of the Navesink River and Atlantic Ocean as you peer over steep coastal cliffs. Just over a mile into the hike, you'll come across the Black Cove Fishing Pier, a popular spot for fishing on the briny waters of the Navesink River. Looking out across the broad expanse of water, you'll see the distant trees of the Sea Bright Peninsula separating the river from the Atlantic Ocean. To the right of the pier is a small sandy beach for relaxing beside the waters, although swimming is not permitted. After walking along the fishing pier, you'll climb up a hillside for a final view of the river and distant ocean via a short loop. At the end of the Rocky Point Trail, you'll take the paved Battery Path for a loop around the military structures.

Although the park is named for a peaceful English Quaker family who settled here in the late 1600s, the area became a strategic military defense site due to its high elevation over the river and its close proximity to New York City. During World War II, the site became dotted with huge concrete batteries for heavy artillery to defend New York Harbor while also serving as underground bunkers to store equipment and protect military personnel. Taking the short loop around the Battery Lewis, you'll explore the bunker and batteries, complete with a 68-foot long gun barrel. If you go on a summer weekend, look out for volunteer-led tours of the remains of the military structures.

## TURN-BY-TURN DIRECTIONS

1. From the parking lot, get on the paved Battery Loop Bike Trail marked by blue squares on signposts.
2. At 0.1 miles, at a T-junction, leave the Battery Loop and continue straight onto the Rocky Point Trail, marked by black diamonds on trees.
3. At 0.7 miles, turn left to the Rocky Point Trail overlook. After enjoying the overlook views, double back to continue on the Rocky Point Trail.
4. At 1.2 miles, at an intersection, turn left onto the unmarked paved trail leading down the hill to the fishing pier. Once you've explored the pier, return up the hill back to the intersection and turn left to continue on the Rocky Point Trail.
5. At 1.8 miles, continue straight on the Rocky Point Trail, ignoring an unmarked trail on the right.
6. At 1.9 miles, turn left to complete a 0.2 mile lollipop loop around the scenic viewpoint. The loop ends in the same spot and then continues on the Rocky Point Trail.
7. At 2.5 miles, cross over a paved bike trail.
8. At 2.7 miles, turn right into the parking lot. Pass the restrooms and get on the Battery Loop Trail toward the historic area.
9. At 3.0 miles, loop around the historic battery, then head back to the parking lot.

## FIND THE TRAILHEAD

From Keyport, get on NJ-36 S. Be prepared for beach traffic in the summer. After around 10 miles, turn right onto Miller Road. Immediately after turning, turn left onto Highland Street. After 300 feet, turn right on S. Peak Street. After 1.5 miles, turn right on Portland Road and then enter the park parking lot with a sign for Monmouth County Parks. The paved trail begins just to the left of the car entrance.

# CARTON BREWING CO.

It's all in the family at Carton Brewing! Cousins Chris and Augie Carton were born and raised in the Bayshore Region and the Atlantic Highlands was the only place the two wanted to open their craft brewery. Located in an old brick warehouse, you'll find the brewhouse and retail store on the ground floor. Head upstairs and you'll find yourself in an eclectic living room, complete with quirky art and comfy sofas. Bars on either side of the room are fully stocked with Caron's unique offerings such as the Carton of Milk Stout. Called a "session nitro stout," it packs all the creaminess of a milk stout into a cool 4% ABV. The perfect beachy dark beer!

## LAND MANAGER

**Monmouth County Park System**
805 Newman Springs Road
Lincroft, New Jersey 07738
(732) 842-4000
www.monmouthcountyparks.com
Map: www.monmouthcountyparks.com/documents/130/
Hartshorne-Map-Webpdf.pdf

## BREWERY/RESTAURANT

**Carton Brewery**
6 E Washington Avenue
Atlantic Highlands, NJ 07716
(732) 654-2337
www.cartonbrewing.com

Distance from trailhead: 4 miles

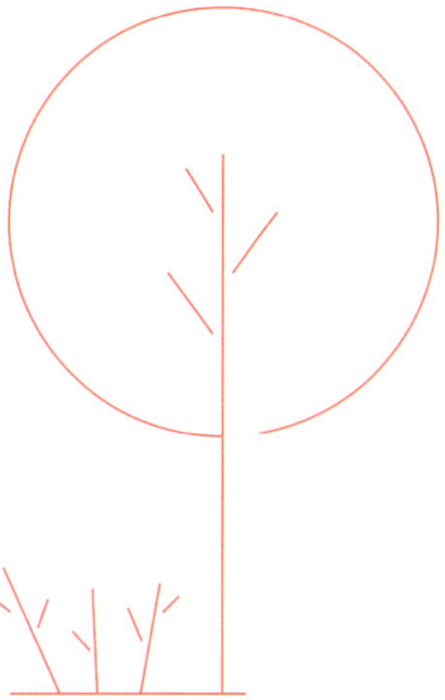

# BATSTO LAKE

## A SCENIC LAKE IN THE HEART OF THE PINELANDS

| STARTING POINT | DESTINATION |
|---|---|
| BATSTO VISITORS CENTER | BATSTO LAKE |
| BREWERY | HIKE TYPE |
| VINYL BREWING CO. | EASY |
| DOG-FRIENDLY | SEASON |
| YES (LEASH REQUIRED) | YEAR-ROUND |
| FEES | DURATION |
| NONE | 2 HOURS |
| MAP REFERENCE | LENGTH |
| POSTED AT TRAILHEAD | 4.2 MILES (LOOP) |
| HIGHLIGHTS | ELEVATION GAIN |
| PINE BARRENS, WILDLIFE | 131 FEET |

**6.0 %**
ALCOHOL CONTENT

## MY BRAIN HURTS IPA

TANGERINE

HOP-FORWARD

LIGHTLY CITRUS

BITTERNESS

SWEETNESS

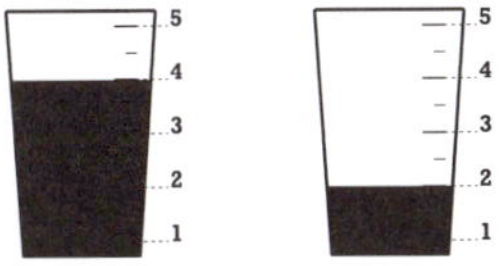


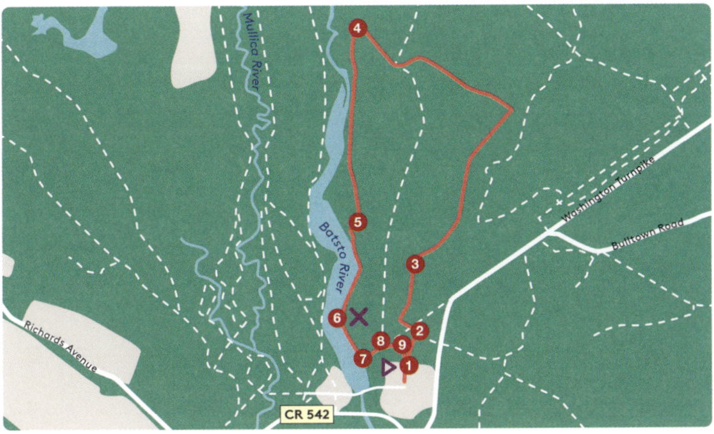


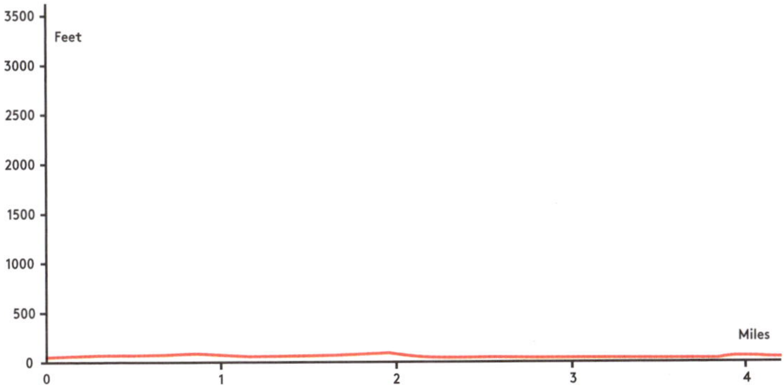

# HIKE DESCRIPTION

**Hike through the pine barrens of Wharton State Forest in the blueberry capital of the world. Afterward, head to Main Street Hammonton for a taste of small-town living at the groovy Vinyl Brewing Co.**

Your hike begins at the Batsto Village visitor center where you'll find an exhibit about the unique ecology of the 1.1 million-acre Pinelands in South Jersey. Besides the hiking trails in the state forest, there's also a living history museum on site about the early Swedish inhabitants of the Batsto Area. From the visitor center, you'll cross the parking lot toward the picnic area where the hiking trails begin. Along this trek, you'll often be hiking along shared trails so they will have two or more color blazes. When you first start, you'll be on a trail marked with blue and white blazes, signaling it's part of both of these trails. As soon as the sandy trail passes from the picnic area into the pine trees, it meets an intersection with the long-distance Batona Trail, marked with pink blazes. This 50-mile trail travels through South Jersey, beginning in Brendan T. Byrne State Forest and ending in Bass River State Forest.

As you walk through the pine trees, you'll notice quite a few burned-down stumps and trunks marked with ash. Fire plays an integral role in the ecology of the Pinelands. Frequent forest fires burn through the dry, sandy soil and flammable vegetation. The pitch pine trees of the barrens have adapted to this fire cycle by using the heat of the flames to release seeds from their tightly sapped cones. After a fire, the pine trees are some of the first plants to emerge from the ashes. As you continue through the pine forest, notice how some areas have burned more recently than others.

Along the way, you'll see that there is little variation in the plant life. The breaking down of pine needles and bark creates highly acidic soil that most vegetation can't grow in. However, wild blueberry bushes

dominate the undergrowth in Wharton State Forest because they specifically requireacidic soil to flourish. White flowers dot the bushes in the spring and the tasty fruits ripen by mid-summer. Blueberries grow so prolifically in the region that the nearby town of Hammonton is known as the blueberry capital of the world.

After meandering in the young pine forest for about two and a half miles, you'll leave the pink-blazed Batona Trail and continue on the White Trail as it turns to follow along the Batsto River. You'll notice that the woods to the right have not suffered the same level of burn as the woods you just left. Ahead, Batsto Lake is visible through the trees. Along this part of the trail, you'll find various benches where you can sit and take in the scenery over the lake. About three and a half miles into the journey, you'll join the Red Trail, a nature path with interpretive signs about the Pine Barrens ecosystem. The path alternates between dirt paths and raised boardwalks over acidic bogs. Keep your eyes peeled for pitcher plants and mosses that flourish in the boggy waters.

The boardwalks let out onto a gravel road. You'll pass a maintenance shed, then go to the right of the fence to get back on the wooded path. This path leads back to the picnic area and the visitor center parking lot.

## TURN-BY-TURN DIRECTIONS

1. From the visitor center, head north through the parking lot toward the picnic area. Pass a trailhead kiosk, then turn right to begin on the shared Blue and White Trail.
2. At 0.2 miles, turn left at the T-junction to get on the pink-blazed Batona Trail, which is marked by a large wooden sign. The trail is still shared by the Blue and White Trails.
3. At 0.6 miles, at the Y-junction, the Batona and White Trail splits from the Blue Trail; turn right to stay on the Batona and White Trail.
4. At 2.3 miles, turn left onto the White Trail, leaving the Batona Trail. To the left, bogs and the Batsto River are down the hillside.
5. At 3.2 miles, keep right as the White Trail meets back up with the Blue Trail and gradually descends toward the lakeside.
6. At 3.6 miles, the White and Blue Trail meet up with the Red Trail. Continue straight along the lakeside path using the boardwalks to cross over the bogs.
7. At 3.8 miles, turn left onto a dirt road, leaving behind Batsto Lake, but remaining on the shared White, Blue, and Red Trail.
8. At 3.9 miles, reach a large gate. Get on the single-track path heading to the right of the gate and leaving the White Trail. You are now on the Blue and Red Trail.
9. At 4.1 miles, the Blue and Red Trail returns to the picnic area from Step 1. Continue through the parking lot and back to the visitor center.

# FIND THE TRAILHEAD

From the town of Hammonton, get on Central Avenue heading east. Proceed for 1.6 miles; then turn right at the traffic light onto South White Horse Pike. Get in the far left lane and immediately make a left at the light onto Pleasant Mills Road. Continue for 2.3 miles, at which point Pleasant Mills Road becomes Nesco Road. Proceed on Nesco Road for another 4 miles. When Nesco Road crosses over Pleasant Mills Road (a different road from before), it becomes Hammonton Road. After 0.9 miles, turn left onto Batsto Road, following the large sign for Batsto Historic Site and Wharton State Forest. Follow Batsto Road for 0.3 miles; then turn left at the sign for Batsto Village Parking. The parking lot will be on the left in 300 feet. The trail begins at the Batsto Visitor's Center, the large building to the left of the parking lot.

# VINYL BREWING CO.

Vinyl Brewing Co. is the brainchild of music enthusiast and brewer Jim Sacco. After over a decade of brewing professionally and at home, Jim decided to launch his own business. With the help of his aunt and uncle, Tom and Susan Puentes, the brewery and taproom opened in Hammonton in 2017. Located right in the center of the business district, the inviting taproom is surrounded by shops and restaurants. The roll-up garage doors invite passersby to stop in for a pint. The hip taproom was designed by Jim's cousin Liz Puentes and the walls are decked out with music memorabilia and posters. Jim, Susan, and Tom did all the renovations themselves. In fact, Tom built the giant U-shaped bar that anchors the whole space by hand. Once a brewery desert, Hammonton is now dubbed "Brewmuda Triangle" for having three breweries in town, a first for South Jersey.

Jim is a small-batch brewer so the taps are always rotating to something new at Vinyl. However, one IPA that Jim keeps coming back to is the My Brain Hurts IPA. It's the perfect middle ground between a Hazy IPA and a West Coast IPA. A slightly citrus sweetness helps to offset the hoppy bitterness for a balanced draft, ideal for sipping while jamming to punk rock in the taproom.

## LAND MANAGER

**Wharton State Forest**
31 Batsto Road
Hammonton, NJ 08037
(609) 561-0024
nj.gov/dep/parksandforests/parks/whartonstateforest.html
Map: nj.gov/dep/parksandforests/maps/wharton-area.pdf

## BREWERY/RESTAURANT

**Vinyl Brewing Co.**
300 12th Street
Hammonton, NJ 08037
(609) 666-5460
www.vinylbrewingnj.com

Distance from trailhead: 9.2 miles

# MAURICE RIVER BLUFFS

## WILDLIFE ABOUNDS IN THIS RIVERSIDE NATURE PRESERVE

| STARTING POINT | DESTINATION |
|---|---|
| NATURE CONSERVANCY KIOSK | MAURICE RIVER DOCK |
| **BREWERY** | **HIKE TYPE** |
| GLASSTOWN BREWING CO. | MODERATE |
| **DOG-FRIENDLY** | **SEASON** |
| YES (LEASH REQUIRED) | YEAR-ROUND |
| **FEES** | **DURATION** |
| NONE | 2 HOURS |
| **MAP REFERENCE** | **LENGTH** |
| POSTED AT TRAILHEAD | 5.0 MILES (LOOP) |
| **HIGHLIGHTS** | **ELEVATION GAIN** |
| RIVER DOCK, HISTORIC RUINS | 250 FEET |

**4.8%**
ALCOHOL CONTENT

## FORTESCUE FISHERMAN'S ALE

COPPERY BROWN

SWEET AND HOPPY

LIGHTLY SWEET BISCUIT

**BITTERNESS**

**SWEETNESS**

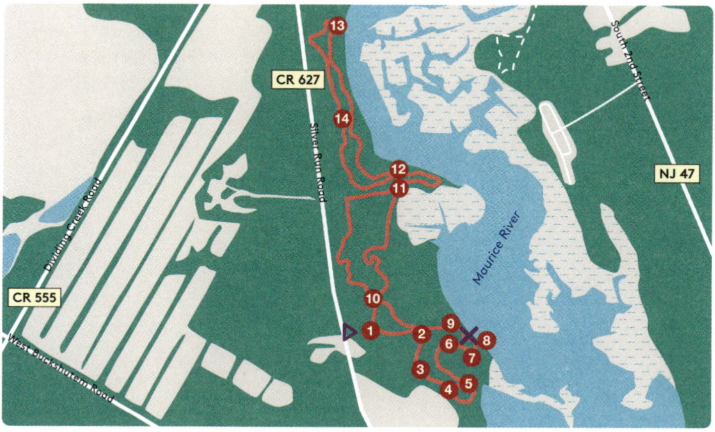


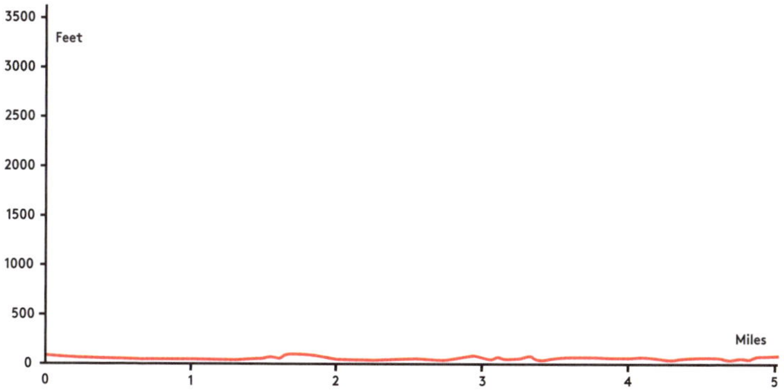

# HIKE DESCRIPTION

**Ramble through this hidden gem in Southern Jersey with miles of wetland habitat and flushes of wildflowers. Afterward, enjoy a pint at the cozy Glasstown Brewing Co. taproom.**

The Nature Conservancy protects over 500 acres along the Maurice River, which drains into the Delaware Bay and provides a critical habitat for migrating birds and fish. The preserve is known for its impressive sandy bluffs overlooking the water. Plus, it touts a hiking trail system of over 5 miles and a bike system of 6 miles. The two trail systems are separate but often cross over one another and can get confusing, so it's useful to have a map handy. This route takes you along intersecting loops to complete several color-coded hiking systems in the park.

Towering pine trees shade the start on the Blue Trail, while the sandy soil and pine needles underfoot create a soft path. From the Blue Trail, you'll transition to a loop on the Orange Trail, which has stunning viewpoints out over the marshlands. The main one is a bird blind, where you can observe waterfowl and raptors without being seen by the birds. After finishing the Orange Loop, you'll return to the Blue Trail to head down toward the river bed. Along this trail, you'll pass by the ruins of an old farmstead; it's one of the few remnants of the area's past as fruit and vegetable farmland before the Nature Conservancy purchased it in 1992. Make sure to only view the ruins from the trail as the area surrounding the ruins is a delicate wildlife area. Heading down to the tree-lined riverbed, it doesn't seem possible that the area was also once a major granary, with barges transporting the chicken feed down the river. Now, the protected marshland along the river provides an excellent habitat for bald eagles and ospreys. Be sure to carry some binoculars to observe osprey nests along the river.

After enjoying some birdwatching, you'll pick up the Blue Trail again and walk along the river bluffs for about a quarter mile. A part of the main Blue Trail closes from January to July for nesting birds. For this route, we'll opt to take the Blue Alternate Trail that's open year-round, but depending on when you hike, you may have a choice between the main Blue Trail and the alternate. Soon after, you'll get on the wooded Red Trail, a prime spot for seeing spring wildflowers like the stunning pink lady slipper orchid. The Red Trail connects to the final two loops of the hike: the White and Yellow. The White Trail is only a quarter-mile long and leads to a stunning river overlook on a sandy outcropping. The longer Yellow Trail passes water viewpoints and industrial remains from when people mined the river bed for sand. At the halfway point on the Yellow Trail, you'll descend a hillside to an artesian well. This is a type of pumpless well that perpetually brings groundwater to the surface. Yes, you can fill up a water bottle here without needing a filter! Once you close out the Yellow Loop and get back on the Red Trail, you'll head away from the river, passing little ponds popular with American bullfrogs and eastern painted turtles. If you sneak by, you may glimpse the turtles basking on a log before finishing up the hike back on the Blue Trail.

## TURN-BY-TURN DIRECTIONS

1. From the parking lot, proceed to the colorful arch with large maps and wildlife displays. The trail splits in two directions; take the right branch of the Blue Trail.
2. At 0.2 miles, turn right at the trail intersection onto the Orange Trail marked by a signpost.
3. At 0.4 miles, turn right again, continuing on the Orange Trail.
4. At 0.5 miles, take the left branch of the Orange Trail up the stairs to start a loop.
5. At 0.8 miles, complete the loop, then turn left to continue on the Orange Trail.
6. At 1.0 miles, turn right at the T-junction to get on the Blue Trail. In 300 feet, pass the ruins on the right side of the trail.
7. At 1.1 miles, turn left to stay on the Blue Trail, ignoring the left trail, which leads to private property.
8. At 1.2 miles, the Blue Trail leads down a hillside to a kayak launch and a floating dock on the river. After exploring, go back up the hill to continue on the Blue Trail.
9. At 1.4 miles, turn left to leave behind the main Blue Trail and take the Blue Alternate Trail.
10. At 1.7 miles, reach a 4-way trail intersection with the Blue and Red Trails. Turn right onto the combined Red and Blue Trail. In 300 feet, continue straight on the Red Trail, leaving the blue blazes behind.
11. At 2.3 miles, at a 4-way trail intersection, turn right onto the White Trail, a short loop of the river bluffs.
12. At 2.6 miles, complete the White Trail, then turn right to get on the Yellow Trail loop.
13. At 3.4 miles, reach a potable water well.
14. At 3.9 miles, stay to the right on the Yellow Trail, do not take the left hand yellow shortcut trail.
15. At 4.3 miles, the Yellow Trail loop ends at an intersection with the White Trail, the same junction from Step 12. Turn right and follow the White Trail for 100 feet before turning right on the Red Trail.
16. At 4.9 miles, encounter the same intersection from Step 10. This time, turn right to get on the final section of the Blue Trail to return to the parking lot.

# FIND THE TRAILHEAD

From Route 55-S in Millville, take Exit 24 for NJ-49E toward Millville. Stay in the right lane and turn right at the stop sign onto NJ-49E/ Main Street. Proceed for 1.8 miles, then turn left at the traffic light onto Cedar Street. Continue on Cedar Street for 0.2 miles, then turn left at the traffic light onto South Race Street. In 0.4 miles, South Race becomes Silver Run Road. Continue on Silver Run Road for 2.3 miles. The Nature Preserve will be on the left, marked by a large green sign. Pull onto the sandy road and keep to the right to enter the parking lot.

# GLASSTOWN BREWING CO.

As one of the early craft brewery owners in New Jersey, Jen and Paul Simmons know a thing or two about beer. Originally from Cape May County, the couple now live in Millville. When they started their brewery in 2013, it was only the 13th brewery in New Jersey. While they've grown to a much larger capacity in the years since, Paul keeps the original 5-gallon keg from their homebrewing days in the taproom. It sits above the tap list as a reminder of how far the brewery has come.

With their brewery's name, Jen and Paul pay homage to the history of Millville. The large amounts of silica found in the sand made Millville one of the biggest glass producers in the country. Thus, it earned the moniker Glasstown. The couple also draws from local culture and history for many of their beer names. For example, the local area phone codes provide the name for both the headliner IPA and DIPA. The Fortescue Fisherman's Ale is a light and malty brew that Paul brewed as a nod to the local fishermen who support the economy of South Jersey.

The taproom is located at the tiny Millville Airport. The unconventional location means you can sip a brew while watching helicopters and small planes take off.

## LAND MANAGER

**The Nature Conservancy (New Jersey)**
200 Pottersville Road
Chester, NJ 07930
(908) 879-7262
www.nature.org/en-us/about-us/where-we-work/united-states/new-jersey
Map: www.nature.org/content/dam/tnc/nature/en/documents/MauriceRiverBluffs-trail-RELEASE.pdf

## BREWERY/RESTAURANT

**Glasstown Brewing Co.**
10 Peterson Street
Millville, NJ 08332
(856) 327-7770
www.glasstownbrewery.com

Distance from Trailhead: 3.7 miles

# CAPE MAY POINT

## HIKE ALONG A BOARDWALK TO SANDY BEACHES

| STARTING POINT | DESTINATION |
|---|---|
| CAPE MAY POINT VISITOR CENTER | BEACH |
| **BREWERY** | **HIKE TYPE** |
| CAPE MAY BREWING CO. | EASY |
| **DOG-FRIENDLY** | **SEASON** |
| NO | YEAR-ROUND |
| **FEES** | **DURATION** |
| NONE | 1 HOUR |
| **MAP REFERENCE** | **LENGTH** |
| POSTED AT TRAILHEAD | 2.2 MILES (LOOP) |
| **HIGHLIGHTS** | **ELEVATION GAIN** |
| BOARDWALKS, BIRDING, OCEAN | 25 FEET |

8.0%
ALCOHOL CONTENT

## PINEAPPLE CRUSHIN' IT IPA

GOLD

TROPICAL FRUIT

TART, HOPPY

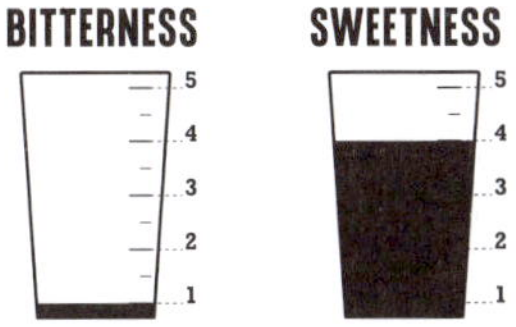


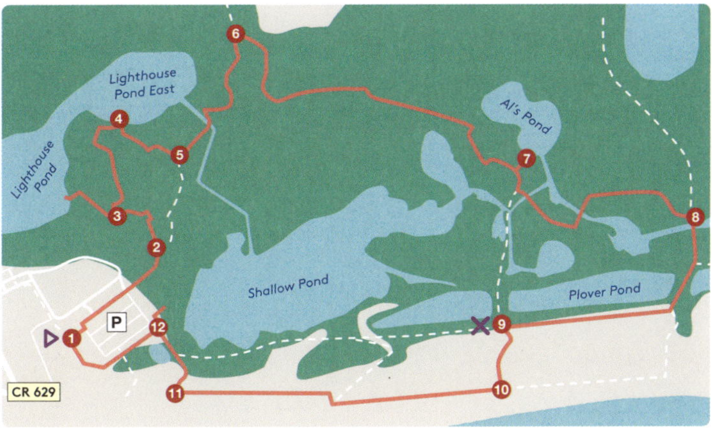


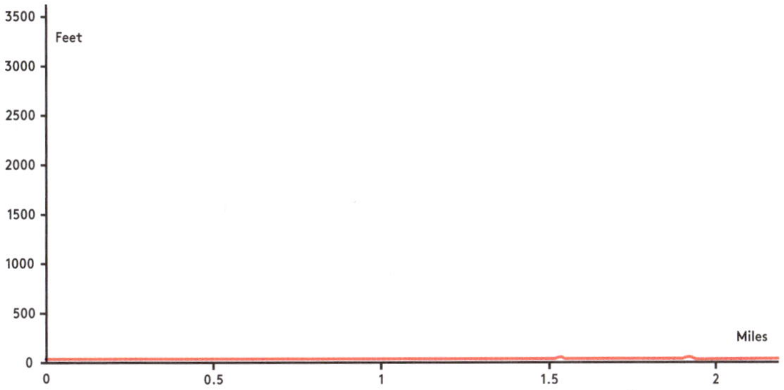

# HIKE DESCRIPTION

**Explore an oceanfront park prized for its natural landscape and abundance of migrating birds. Posthike, take a load off at Cape May Brewing Co. where every day feels like summer vacation.**

Cape May Point State Park is at the southernmost tip of New Jersey where the Delaware Bay meets the Atlantic Ocean. Forests, freshwater marshes, and ocean beaches make the park a haven for migrating birds. Between boardwalks and flat wooded trails, the hike is perfect for all experience levels. Due to the delicate nature of the ecosystem here, dogs are not permitted on the trails.

You'll start this hike on the wide boardwalk at the far side of the parking lot. Along the way, there are educational signs about the various types of plant life. Even in the sandy soil so close to the ocean, you'll find a mix of tall trees like eastern red cedar and pitch pines, while

bayberries and wax myrtles fill the undergrowth. Just after starting, you'll loop around the freshwater Lighthouse Ponds on the Duck Pond Trail. You'll find two observation platforms along the loop where you can pause and take in the ducks, wading birds, bald eagles, and even otters that make their homes here. Continuing along the boardwalk, you'll pass several smaller ponds where you might spot turtles and water snakes.

After the Duck Pond Trail, the path alternates between boardwalks surrounded by marshes and reed grasses, and sandy paths through pitch pine groves. About a mile into the trek, you'll reach another observation point to gaze out over a freshwater pond tucked into an oak and hickory grove. After the pond, the trail comes out of the forest and the Cape May Lighthouse emerges in the distance. The twin Plover Ponds, home to a pair of swans, are directly ahead. You'll continue along the path as it hugs the shore of the ponds before heading up the dune path toward the white expanse of beach. Be mindful that areas of the beach are seasonally closed for nesting birds; oystercatchers, piping plovers, and least terns hunt for their next meal along the shore. You'll walk along the sand toward the concrete bunker in the distance that was once a WWII military site. The crumbling concrete behemoth is all that remains from a time before the beach was preserved for wildlife.

After passing the bunker, you'll head toward the dunes to get on a boardwalk leading to the parking lot, but you're not quite done yet. To the right of where the trails started, there's a large wooden observation structure. This platform is specifically for observing hawks and other birds of prey. With a unique geographic location between two major bodies of water, Cape May Point is a fantastic location to view migrating birds. Helpful identifying images of raptors line the railings of the platform. With a bit of patience and luck, you might see one of these majestic soaring hunters.

## TURN-BY-TURN DIRECTIONS

1. From the visitor center, cross the parking lot to the start of the boardwalk marked by a large brown sign for the Nature Area Trails.
2. At 0.1 miles, turn left, following the red-marked Duck Pond Trail.
3. At 0.2 miles, turn left to follow the boardwalk to the bird blind on a pond. Return along the boardwalk, then turn left to continue on the Duck Pond Trail.
4. At 0.4 miles, turn left to another observation platform on the pond. Return along the boardwalk, then turn left to continue on the trail.
5. At 0.5 miles, turn left onto the yellow/blue-blazed Plover and Monarch Trails boardwalk.
6. At 0.7 miles, turn right to continue along the trail, leaving the boardwalk; do not go left onto private property.
7. At 1.0 miles, turn left to another small pondside observation deck. Return to the trail and in 75 feet, turn left to stay on the blue-blazed Plover Trail leaving the yellow Monarch Trail behind.
8. At 1.3 miles, reach a T-junction; turn left and continue along the Plover Trail as it loops around the pond.
9. At 1.5 miles, turn left onto the Beach Access route heading up into the dunes and letting out onto the wide sandy beach.
10. At 1.6 miles, turn right and walk along the beach, passing by the ruins of a military bunker.
11. At 1.9 miles, turn left to leave the beach via the boardwalk path through the dunes. In 200 feet, return to the parking lot and then climb the observation platform overlooking a large pond.
12. At 2.1 miles, after exploring the viewing platform, cross back over the parking lot to end the loop at the Visitor's Center.

# FIND THE TRAILHEAD

From the Cape May Court House, take the Garden State Parkway South and continue for 11 miles. Then, take Exit 0 on the right toward NJ-109. After 0.6 miles, stay in the right turning lane at the intersection, following signs for US-9 South. In 400 feet, go straight at the traffic light to get onto US-9 South. Proceed for 0.4 miles; then, turn left at the light onto Seashore Road. After 2.5 miles, turn right at the light onto Sunset Boulevard. In 1.7 miles, turn left onto Light House Avenue. After 0.7 miles, turn left into the park parking lot by the large brown sign and the lighthouse. The trail begins on the opposite side of the parking lot from the lighthouse by the brown trail sign for "Nature Area."

# CAPE MAY BREWING CO.

Cape May Brewing Co. was born during a summer weekend in 2010 when three friends did a homebrew kit together on the Jersey Shore. Ryan Krill, his friend and former college roommate Chris "Hank" Henke, and Ryan's dad Bob Krill thought the brew was pretty good and joked about starting a brewery. All jokes aside, within a year, the three delivered their first keg of Cape May IPA to a beach bar in Cape May and it was a hit. By 2011, they secured a brewing space at the Cape May Airport to start their new venture. At the time, breweries were new to New Jersey, with Cape May Brewing being only the 15th in the state. Fast forward to now, the three-person team has grown to over 130 people and is now the largest craft brewery in the state.

Don't let the size of this powerhouse brewery intimidate you though—the Cape May Taproom is a warm and inviting space reminiscent of a beachside cabana. When you walk in, check out the self-guided tour explaining the brewing process and sharing fun tidbits about the brewery. Then, you can either enjoy your beer in the buzzing taproom or out in the beer garden where there's often live music.

The taproom offers a huge lineup of house-made brews as well as some seltzers and hard lemonades. Always on tap are headliners and fan-favorites like the Cape May IPA and The Bog Cranberry Shandy, as well as rotating experimental drafts. Born out of a friendly homebrew competition among the brewery staff, the Crushin' It Series grew into a popular summer tropical series. The Pineapple Crushin' It is a full-bodied hazy IPA with tropical flavors that are begging to be enjoyed with your feet in the sand.

## LAND MANAGER

**Cape May Point State Park**
303 County Highway 629
Cape May, NJ 08204
(609) 884-2159
nj.gov/dep/parksandforests/parks/capemaypointstatepark.html
Map: nj.gov/dep/parksandforests/maps/capemaypoint-area.pdf

## BREWERY/RESTAURANT

**Cape May Brewing Co.**
1250 Hornet Road
Rio Grande, NJ 08242
(609) 849-9933
www.capemaybrewery.com

Distance from trailhead: 7.4 miles

# ACKNOWLEDGEMENTS

This book would not have been possible without the boundless support of my husband and hiking partner Justin. Thank you for driving me around nearly every weekend and always remembering to take notes at the brewery when I got too invested in the conversation to do so. I'm so glad that we discovered the joys of hiking together. There's no one else I'd rather spend hours in the woods with looking for a "pretty good tree."

To Elaine and Tom Devlin, who first introduced me to craft beer and have been endless supporters of Hikes & Hops since the very beginning, I've cherished every minute of getting to introduce you to my favorite trails.

There are not enough words to express my gratitude to editor Johanna Flashman for taking on a completely novice writer and patiently whipping this book into shape. This book would have been in shambles without your eagle eye and support, especially when I felt out of my depth.

Sincere thanks to the Helvetiq team who have made my writing dreams come true. To Richard Harvell, who continued to reach out even though I thought his email wasn't real. So much gratitude to Daniel Malak for his beautiful work on the stunning maps and graphics in the book. I'm sorry I'm so bad at photographing beer glasses.

To everyone that hosted me during my many trips across the state, including the Parisi family who generously shared their family cabin during one of my trips. Huge thanks to Kat and Matt Nicholas who not only housed and fed me during a Philly trip, but also provided invaluable advice about their favorite breweries. Thanks to my book club ladies, Claire, Shyleigh, Michelle, and Emma, for letting me hijack a girls weekend for a hiking trip.

To Tory Mather, for our weekly writing sessions. I never would have finished this without your endless cheerleading and listening to me wax poetic about this book for over a year. I can't wait to read your book next!

To the Pittsburgh Trail Sisters running group, who have been anxiously awaiting this publication and joined me for the final hike and a celebratory beer.

To Carey Kish, author of Beer Hiking New England, who made time to chat with a newbie writer and convinced me to take on this project: you were right, this was so worth it.

To all the followers of Hikes & Hops, thank you for your support of my little blog that made this opportunity possible! I never could have imagined that so many people would be interested in my travels and weekend adventures.

A hearty thank you to all the brewers, owners, managers, and more that made time out of their busy schedules to share a beer with me and talk about their businesses. I heard so many fascinating stories and am so impressed with your gumption and commitment to your craft!

And finally, to all of the incredible park rangers, trail maintenance staff, and volunteers who work hard every day to preserve the great outdoors for all of us. Let's never take for granted the hours of behind-the-scenes work that goes into making these trails and parks accessible for all of us.

# GO BEER HIKING!

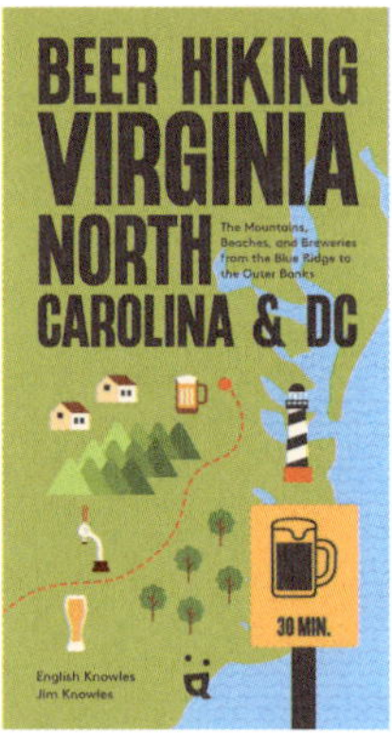


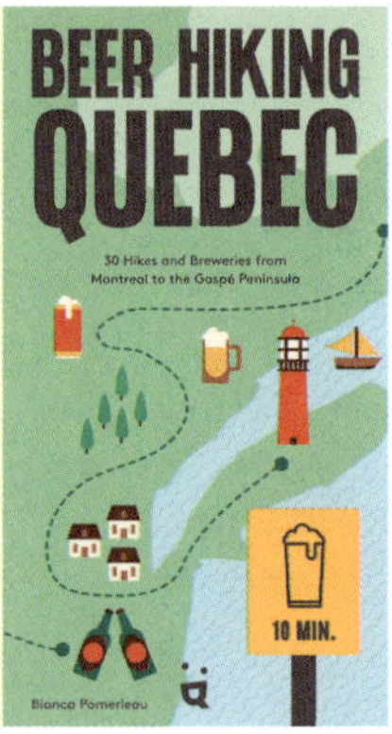